Troy Duster

Troy Duster

Troy Duster

Berkeley Sociologist, Teacher, and Civil Rights Activist

John F. Galliher

Hamilton Books

An Imprint of
Rowman & Littlefield
Lanham • Boulder • New York • Toronto • Plymouth, UK

Copyright © 2016 by Hamilton Books
4501 Forbes Boulevard, Suite 200, Lanham, Maryland 20706
Hamilton Books Acquisitions Department (301) 459-3366

Unit A, Whitacre Mews, 26-34 Stannary Street,
London SE11 4AB, United Kingdom

Library of Congress Control Number: 2015953514
ISBN: 978-0-7618-6700-5 (pbk : alk. paper)—ISBN: 978-0-7618-6701-2 (electronic)

∞™ The paper used in this publication meets the minimum requirements of American National Standard for Information Sciences Permanence of Paper for Printed Library Materials, ANSI/NISO Z39.48-1992.

Contents

Preface

This book is a biography of African American professor of sociology Troy Duster. Duster received his PhD from Northwestern University in 1962; his dissertation was a social experiment titled *The Social Response to Abnormality*. He spent the majority of his teaching and research career at the University of California, Berkeley, where he became a Chancellor's Professor in 1998. Duster spent the last part of his teaching career at New York University (1999–2012), where he became a Silver Professor of Sociology shortly after arriving there in 1999. He was elected president of the American Sociological Association in 2005.

Since retiring from NYU Troy has been a Senior Fellow at the Warren Institute on Law and Policy at the Boalt School of Law at the University of California, Berkeley, as well as continuing as a Chancellor's Professor at Berkeley. Retaining his appointment as a Chancellor's Professor at Berkeley allowed him to teach and advise as he chooses, during and after his years at NYU.

More important than these accomplishments, however, was Professor Duster's commitment to the concept of "public sociology." Along with several Berkeley academics, Duster sought to practice a sociology that is oriented to seeking just and fair public policy. Although public sociology deals with many other topics than race, Duster's practice of public sociology sets him firmly as a part of a long progression of black American intellectuals, as outlined in William M. Banks's *The Black Intellectuals* (1996).

The Black Intellectuals offers a glimpse into this long tradition of African American thinkers working on behalf of social justice. For example, Frederick Douglass (1817–1895) "urged blacks to fight for human rights" (Banks 1996: 227). Douglass served in the administration of President Lincoln and argued for the rights of not only blacks but also women, as did Professor

Duster. There is also Anna J. Cooper, who was born a slave in North Carolina in 1858 and died in 1964 in Washington, DC. In her book *A View from the South* (1988) she argued that whites do not value African culture and that black Americans, through no fault of their own, find themselves today the inheritor of a manhood and womanhood impoverished and debased by two centuries of degradation" (1988: 28). Then there is the famous Ida B. Wells (1862–1931), who was a pioneering antilynching journalist. As it happens she also deserves special attention because she was the maternal grandmother of Troy Duster. Ms. Wells was born a slave in Mississippi in 1862 and died in Chicago in 1931. She worked as a journalist in Memphis where she routinely opposed lynching (Wells 1970). She reported that "the Southerner had never gotten over his resentment that the Negro was no longer his plaything, his servant, and his source of income" (1970: 70). "I found that in order to justify these horrible atrocities [directed against African Americans] to the world, the Negro was being branded as a race of rapists, who were especially mad after white women" (1970: 71). Ida B. Wells was critical of the efforts of Southern whites as well as Northern whites for the continuance of lynching. She was also critical of U.S. presidents who turned a blind eye to race riots, including the slaughter of 150 African Americans during two days of rioting in East Saint Louis, Illinois.

Banks traces the history of other black American intellectuals as well. W.E.B. DuBois (1868–1963) observed rural black life and praised its humility, perseverance, and religiosity. In 1935 he publicly condemned both racism and fascism. DuBois also called for voting rights for African Americans, college educations and full employment, as guaranteed to white Americans (Peterson 2007). According to DuBois the long, sad history of black lynching, their disfranchisement and their unemployment have all left African Americans "in a fighting mood" (Lewis 2000: 6). He was a communist who believed that race prejudice against Japanese was partially responsible for WWII (Horne 1986).

Another black intellectual in this tradition was E. Franklin Frazier (1894–1962), president of the American Sociological Society in 1948. In *Black Bourgeoisie*, he noted that the black elites often had both a disdain for poor blacks and a guilty conscience for this attitude (Frazier 1957). We will see that Troy Duster has nothing in common with the black elites described by Frazier. And yet Duster, as a Berkeley professor, was aware of the complexities of what Eric Brown, in his book *The Black Professional Middle Class,* called the "truly advantaged" (Brown 2014). These black professionals suffered their own challenges, such as being excluded from elite country clubs on the basis of their race.

Brown's book studied the experience of black professionals in Oakland, California. He found that during the early 1900s, the few black professionals in Oakland had a client list made up almost exclusively of the small black middle class, mostly teachers and attorneys. Later in the century migration of more blacks into the area intensified opposition to their presence in Oakland; Brown noted that from 1960 to 2000 the proportion of blacks increased approximately five times, and late in the century black politician Lionel Wilson was a four-term mayor of the city.

Banks discusses other black intellectuals including Langston Hughes (1902–1967), who was unassuming but wrote about fifty books, including a two-volume autobiography. Richard Wright (1908–1960) was for a time a member of the communist party. Bayard Rustin (1910–1987) was also at one time a member of the communist party and of the Congress of Racial Equality (CORE), and he was the cofounder of the Southern Christian Leadership Conference (SCLC). Kenneth Clark (born in 1914) served as president of the American Psychological Association in 1970–1971 and worked on research used by the U.S. Supreme Court in the 1954 *Brown v. Board of Education of Topeka* decision outlawing racial segregation. Banks mentions John Hope Franklin (born in 1915) who was the first black to head the Southern Historical Association and also the American Historical Association, as well as author Henry Louis Gates Jr. (born 1950).

All of these thinkers and writers helped to form Troy Duster's intellectual development, as did national events of the 1950s and 1960s. In 1955 Emmett Till was lynched in Mississippi and in 1957 racial conflict regarding opposition to school integration became palpable in Little Rock, Arkansas. In 1963 Dr. Martin Luther King was assassinated in Memphis, and in 1965 there was a massive race riot in Los Angeles. That same year Malcolm X was murdered in Harlem. These are just a few of the major racial disturbances that occurred as Troy Duster was starting his career. In 1978 African American sociologist William J. Wilson published a book *The Declining Significance of Race* arguing that race is less important than it once was in America. We will see that Tory Duster took issue with this position.

This book is intended to detail the course of Troy Duster's career as well as illuminate his contributions to the field of sociology and social justice. It joins several other biographies of sociologists who fought for human rights through the course of the twentieth century. There are volumes on the criminologist Edwin Sutherland (Gaylord and Galliher 1988); the founders of the Society for the Study of Social Problems, Betty and Al Lee, who were sometimes shunned for their leftist criticism of the ASA (Galliher and Galliher 1995); Alfred Lindesmith (Keys and Galliher 2000); and Mabel Elliott, who, like Duster, earned a PhD from Northwestern, hers in 1929 (McGonigal and Galliher 2009). Like Troy Duster all of these figures have some claim to being Midwesterners and an interest in public policy and human rights. And all experienced marginalization and sometimes surveillance by the FBI, as did Duster. Sutherland, Lindesmith, and Elliott had an interest in crime, and Lindesmith was primarily concerned with drug laws. Because she was a woman Mabel Elliott experienced a salary freeze during the Depression of the 1930s. It was reasoned by her colleagues who were all men that a male who had a family to support needed the money more than she did. She was also a target of the FBI due to her criticism of American prisons, which J. Edgar Hoover had described as "country clubs" (McGonigal and Galliher 2009). Alfred Lindesmith had a nineteen-page FBI file because he steadfastly opposed treating drug addiction as a crime as opposed to an illness; his file has been heavily redacted with only the word "espionage" legible (Keys and Galliher 2000: 223). Laud Humphreys (1930–1988) as an early openly gay sociologist, who was hounded by the FBI; his dissertation on sexual encounters in public restrooms tested the limits of ideas regarding the protection of human subjects (Galliher, Brekhus and Keys 2004).

Some of these sociologists had intertwining careers. Lindesmith worked closely as a graduate student at the University of Chicago with Sutherland and with symbolic interactionist Herbert Blumer, who later moved to Berkeley and consequently had a profound impact on Troy Duster. Prominent sociologist Edwin Sutherland also taught briefly at the University of Chicago, 1930–1934, and overlapped with Lindesmith there where they shared an interest in qualitative sociology; Sutherland ultimately brought Lindesmith to Indiana University in 1936 (Gaylord and Galliher 1988). Edwin Sutherland and Alfred McClung Lee also had FBI files (Keen 1999). Sutherland castigated American corporations for their greed and various related crimes. Troy Duster himself had an FBI file that the FBI now claims it cannot find. Duster saw the file before its "disappearance," and noted that it was heavily redacted and merely indicated that he attended anti-Vietnam war rallies.

DATA SOURCES

I drew on several primary and secondary data sources for this project. One of the most important sources was the oral history of Troy Duster conducted by the University of California, Bancroft. The UC Bancroft Library has launched a series of oral histories on its most distinguished faculty, which is an invaluable resource for researchers. I also consulted Duster's own research and publications as well as publications written about Troy Duster (such as Alondra Nelson's essay about Duster in *Public Culture* in 2012). Primary data was also secured from many interviews and emails with Troy Duster, some of his colleagues and former colleagues, and his former graduate student advisees. Although I have written several other biographies, this is the first about a living person. This brings both advantages (e.g., being able to interview the subject) and disadvantages (e.g., the possibility of self-censorship). Although it was not intended, since the book is almost solely focused on faculty and graduate students at the University of California, Berkeley, it also reflects a good bit about the standards and hiring practices of this elite American university.

A special mention needs to be made of the FBI's file on Troy Duster. In a January 1, 2013, email, Duster recalled his earlier access to his own FBI file: "About 30 years ago, I did use the FOI Act to request my file from the FBI, but when I got it back it was both so redacted with blacked-out phrases and names that it was of no interest and no use. I vaguely recall that they had some information on some anti-Vietnam war petitions and meetings, but there was nothing one could sink one's teeth into." Duster had submitted a letter of appeal, with no result, and I myself contacted the FBI on March 15, 2013, to follow up. After a long series of communications, including among attorneys hired to pursue the matter, on October 24, 2013, FBI employee David M. Hardy stated that the Duster FBI file "may have been . . . destroyed" or may have been sent to the National Archives. The National Archives ultimately indicated that they had no records on Troy Duster.

REFERENCES

Banks, William M. 1996. *The Black Intellectuals: Race and Responsibility in American Life*. New York: Norton.
Brown, Eric S. 2014. *The Black Professional Middle Class*. New York: Routledge.
Cooper, Anna J. 1988. *A View from the South*. New York. Oxford University Press.
Duster, Troy. 2012. "An Oral History with Troy Duster," interview conducted by Richard Cándida and Nadine Wilmot, 2002–2003, Regional Oral History Office, The Bancroft Library, University of California, Berkeley.
Frazier, E. Franklin. 1957. *Black Bourgeoisie*. New York: The Free Press.
Galliher, John F., Wayne Brekhus, and David Keys. 2004. *Laud Humphreys: Prophet of Homosexuality and Sociology*. Madison: University of Wisconsin Press.
Galliher, John F., and James M. Galliher. 1995. *Marginality and Dissent in Twentieth-Century American Sociology: The Case of Elizabeth Briant Lee and Alfred McClung Lee*. Albany: SUNY Press.
Gaylord, Mark S., and John F. Galliher. 1988. *The Criminology of Edwin Sutherland*. New Brunswick, NJ: Transaction Books.
Horne, Gerald. 1986. *Black and Red: W.E.B. DuBois and the Afro-American Response to the Cold War, 1944–1963*. Albany: SUNY Press.
Keen, Mike Forrest. 1999. *Stalking the Sociological Imagination: J. Edgar Hoover's Surveillance of American Sociology*. Westport, CT: Greenwood Press.
Keys, David Patrick, and John F. Galliher. 2000. *Confronting the Drug Control Establishment: Alfred Lindesmith as a Public Intellectual*. Albany: SUNY Press.
Lewis, David Levering. 2000. *W.E.B. DuBois: The Fight for the American Century, 1919–1963*. New York: Holt.
McGonigal, Kathryn, and John F. Galliher. 2009. *Mabel Agnes Elliott: Pioneering Feminist, Pacifist Sociologist*. Lanham, MD: Lexington Books.
Nelson, Alondra. 2012. "Troy Duster Interview." *Public Culture* 24: 283–302.
Peterson, Charles F. 2007. *DuBois, Fanon, Cabral: The Margins of Elite Anti-Colonial Leadership*. New York: Lexington Books.
Wells, Ida B. 1970. *Crusade for Justice: The Autobiography of Ida B. Wells*. Chicago: University of Chicago Press.
Wilson, William Julius. 1978. *The Declining Significance of Race*. Chicago: University of Chicago Press.

Acknowledgments

David Matza provided an amazing amount of help in writing this biography of his long-time friend and colleague. Sociologist Eric Brown, who was an advisee of Troy Duster as a graduate student, interviewed several University of California, Berkeley, sociologists and remembered significant players from his years as a graduate student. Former Missouri University professor Dr. Donald Granberg read a recent version of the manuscript and made several helpful comments. Missouri University librarian Nancy Myers provided invaluable assistance in locating materials at various stages of this research. Jeanne Galliher took many of the Berkeley photographs and provided numerous suggestions for the book manuscript. Others gave myriad help who will go unnamed but not un-thanked. We would also be remiss if we did not especially acknowledge Troy Duster, who provided us with many pictures and answered numerous questions.

Chapter One

Childhood

Troy Smith Duster was born on July 11, 1936, in Chicago, Illinois, the youngest of five children. He was born at home and took his first two names from the family doctor, Troy Smith. He had three brothers, Benjamin, Charles, and Donald, and a sister, Alfreda. All of his siblings read a lot and two brothers were valedictorians, as was he; the remaining brother and his sister graduated second in their class. Troy's father attended Indiana State Normal in Terre Haute but worked as a handyman. The family lived in poverty on the near the South Side of Chicago where people were typically either unemployed or did day work cleaning white households. [1] He was born before the advent of the high rises—vertical urban slums. Troy recalled that his family lived at 3239 Prairie Avenue and that it had eventually been razed as a part of an urban renewal effort. [2] Troy and his brothers and sister all went to public schools that were completely segregated. The only non-African American attending his high school was an Asian named Frank Wong, whose family owned a restaurant in the area. Otherwise the high school of 2,000–3,000 was all black. Of Troy's high school graduating class of 225 only three or four went to elite universities. Troy attended the ancient Douglas Elementary School on Calumet Avenue at 32nd Street and the Wendell Phillips High School at 39th and Prairie.

Troy's maternal grandmother and grandfather were part of Chicago's black elite. His grandmother was Ida B. Wells, a famous anti-lynching and civil rights activist, and Troy's mother attended the University of Chicago. [3] Once the Great Depression of the 1930s hit, her family was reduced to poverty. During his first ten to twelve years he and his family sometimes went to Sunday school at the African Methodist Episcopal Church, but Troy's mother never emphasized church as a source of spiritual guidance. Once Troy was twelve years old, attendance became optional.

1

Figure 1.1. Douglas Elementary School.

Figure 1.2. Wendell Phillips High School.

In spite of eschewing religion as a source of spiritual guidance, Troy's mother did take the church seriously and felt that it "was important to be engaged in one of the most important structural and institutional forces in the African American community."[4] She kept matters of her faith to herself. Troy also prefers to do the same. Troy's mother was "tough and authoritarian . . . and rotated all household chores, since obviously male-female distinctions were irrelevant, because there were four boys and a girl." Her children never even considered crossing her. His mother often emphasized that her children should not try to take credit for the achievements of their grandmother, although his grandmother's existence undoubtedly had a considerable impact upon all of the Duster children's outstanding academic performance.

Figure 1.3. Troy Duster as an infant in 1937, with his older sister Alfreda, in 1944 with a black dog, and as a young man. Photos courtesy of Troy Duster.

As it happens, Troy's families had contact with another important black Chicago family: that of Michelle Obama. The first black US First Lady was born on January 17, 1964. Like Troy she was born and reared in the segregated South Side of Chicago, alternatively referred to as the Black Belt, North Mississippi, and Darkie Town.[5] She also was one of the first in her family to go to college. Demonstrating what a small world existed for prominent

African American's in Chicago, the wife of attorney Benjamin Duster (Troy's older brother) was a frequent associate of Michelle's great-great aunt.[6] Michelle's family often went for long Sunday drives. One Sunday the family drove through a neighborhood of mansions where Michelle's father explained that the small houses in back housed black folks who served the white residents.

Michelle's father had a patronage job with the city water plant. At the time the mayor, who controlled all patronage, was Richard J. Daley who was blatantly racist and pro-war. Daley was the mayor from 1955 until his death in 1976. Michelle's parents had high expectations for their children's grades. Accordingly her brother Craig was the valedictorian of his high school class and Michelle was the salutatorian of hers. Like Craig, Michelle was accepted at Princeton. She earned a sociology undergraduate degree at Princeton. She later graduated from Harvard Law School. Although Michelle and Troy were separated in age by over thirty years, Michelle's and Troy's parents' lack of formal higher education, their ambivalent take on religion, and their parental concern with academic excellence was found in both families. Finally the children from both families attended elite private universities.

NOTES

1. Troy Duster, "An Oral History with Troy Duster," interview conducted by Richard Cándida Smith and Nadine Wilmot, 2002–2003, Regional Oral History Office, The Bancroft Library, University of California, Berkeley, 2012.

2. Troy Duster, email to John Galliher, March 28, 2013.

3. Alondra Nelson, "Troy Duster: Interview," *Public Culture* 24 (2012): 283–302.

4. Troy Duster, email to John Galliher, January 1, 2015.

5. Peter Slevin, *Michelle Obama: A Life* (New York: Knopf, 2015).

6. Slevin, *Michelle Obama.*

Chapter Two

College

Northwestern and UCLA

NORTHWESTERN UNIVERSITY

In 1954 Troy began study at Northwestern University, where he was only one of two black students not on an athletic scholarship. At the time Evanston was completely racially segregated, including its barbershops and bowling alleys. On May 11, 1954, someone said to Troy that this was a big day for him because the Supreme Court had just ruled that segregation was illegal; that was when Troy learned of the historical *Brown v. Board of Education of Topeka* decision.

Troy said that it was significant that during those days at Northwestern everything he did was scrutinized as a result of his being black and "quite visible."[1] He was certainly visible to the local police as well. "I also used to get stopped by the police in Evanston, especially in the evenings. One night an officer came up to me and said 'What are you doing here?' I said that I'm a student. He then asked what I was studying. Predictably, he left me alone after I told him I was reading Nietzsche and Kierkegaard and I became known to the Evanston police as the black student who wasn't an athlete."[2]

His social and academic life at Northwestern was, by necessity, shared with fellow white students, since there were so few black students and they were often athletes or musicians. He was one of only seven or eight black students at the university. The first year at Northwestern, Troy lived with the only other black male who was not on an athletic scholarship. He took pride in being an independent since racism in the fraternity system was palpable. One Northwestern fraternity was threatened with expulsion from the national organization for having pledged an Asian student. It was at Northwestern that

5

Troy first heard the term WASPs—White Anglo Saxon Protestants. North-western was a very preppy school and he dressed to fit in there.

Troy spoke a bit about identity issues at that time, for example the role of hair. For Troy, hair was not a feature of self-identity or blackness. Hair is just "your hair."[3] Some people in the Chicago black community straightened their hair using a hot iron. In males this was referred to as a conk, which his mother did not care for in the least. Later at Berkeley Troy worked with a doctoral student who wrote a thesis on the role of hair in the black community (Maxine Craig, "Ain't I A Beauty Queen").

As an undergraduate he worked weekends as a house painter. He also worked as a busboy and changed the bed linens in the dorms. He also had a Pullman Foundation scholarship. Pullman conductors paid for this, which was intended for poor and minority students. It paid for tuition plus a few hundred dollars of spending money. As long as you kept your grades up the support would continue. Troy's Irish Catholic friend Jack Doyle told him about a unionized garbage job that paid approximately twice what he was making at his other jobs. Jack Doyle then came back to him "mortified" and said that he could not work it out because of "racial exclusion."[4]

Another part of Troy's life at Northwestern was his participation in the ROTC program. He recalls:

> I spent three years in the Air Force ROTC training program at Northwestern when I was an undergraduate, but during my senior year the program was dismantled. If that had not happened I would have had to take a position as a commissioned officer. When I finished my bachelor's degree I went straight to graduate school and thus qualified for an educational deferment.[5]

By his junior year enough people knew him that he was asked to run for the student council. In that role he could engage fraternity boys in debates. Around this time Troy decided to change his major to sociology after transferring from the school of journalism. He and several of his friends had become disillusioned with journalism after observing the coverage of a terrible accident on the Chicago elevated train. Although the motorman was suffering and near death, reporters from ABC and CBS intruded on the man in order to cover the story. "My friends and I decided to leave journalism because of this incident."[6] Troy told sociology professor Ray Mack the story, and he invited Troy to become a sociologist since he had already taken several courses in the field and done well. Ray Mack was a professor in his late twenties who acted as a mentor to Troy.[7] The two served on a university committee that dealt with the problems of racism on campus.

UCLA

It was after beginning his studies with Ray Mack that Duster had an opportunity to expand his academic horizons. Troy recalls:

> I was enrolled in [Ray's] undergraduate course in Race Relations. After introducing me to Wendell Bell, Bell offered me a TA at UCLA where he was headed. But after only two years at UCLA and completing the MA, Ray had become department chair at Northwestern and invited me back to pursue the PhD and work with him on a manuscript titled "Patterns of Minority Relations." Ray patted himself on the back, saying that he knew how to pick talent.[8]

Bell told Troy that he "could become the 'Jackie Robinson of sociology,'" and in 1957, after earning his BA at Northwestern in journalism, Troy decided to make the transfer to UCLA to study with him for his MA. On the way to UCLA Troy stopped in Joplin, Missouri, and because of local racism could not locate a motel that would let him spend the night. So he merely slept in his old car at the side of the road but the local police rousted him and said that he must "move on."[9] Once Troy got to UCLA he got his first real introduction to American residential segregation. As a black man he had great difficulty finding a place to rent in Los Angeles. "I would find an apartment that was near campus . . . but it would always, at the last moment, be taken by someone else."[10] This was a common story of racial barriers at the time in the United States. For Troy graduate school at UCLA was a significant transition out of make-believe civil rights activities at Northwest-

Figure 2.1. Troy in 1956 while an undergraduate at Northwestern. Photo courtesy of Troy Duster.

ern. At UCLA he had to face the reality of housing discrimination in Los Angeles.

But at UCLA Troy met Bill Robinson and Harold Garfinkel. Robinson was an expert in statistics who argued that sociology emphasized science far too much and engaged in a false precision. Garfinkel was a charismatic instructor. He was an ethnomethodologist who taught graduate seminars and had been a student of Talcott Parsons student at Harvard. While "Parsons's work stressed the social structural factors that impinge upon individuals and their interactions, Garfinkel placed greater emphasis on fluidity of social life and "the experience of individuals in interaction."[11] Troy took a graduate course from Garfinkel during his MA program at UCLA. Although he never worked with him in research, Troy recognized that Garfinkel was a very important intellectual. As an ethnomethodologist, "for Garfinkel everything was problematic."[12] Garfinkel's work emphasized that human beings create the rules through which their lives are organized, rather than the culture creating the rules for them, thus emphasizing human freedom rather than control. He emphasized the fluidity of social life. Whether you are black, gay, female or French or Jewish, one minute you could be French and another you are Jewish. The value Troy placed on Garfinkel says a good deal about him and would determine the direction of Troy's career. He also studied alongside Egon Bittner. Although Egon was a fellow graduate student he broadened Troy's worldview considerably since he was much older. Egon had been a victim of the Holocaust and had survived Buchenwald.

RETURN TO NORTHWESTERN

To complete his graduate studies Troy went back to Northwestern to work with Ray Mack, John Kitsuse, and Aaron Cicourel. Ray Mack was now the department chair and Ray had a fellowship from the Ford Foundation awaiting him.[13] Ray Mack was Troy's dissertation supervisor, and Troy focused his work on how the families of the mentally ill cope with this condition. He designed a study that gathered five or six people in a room, only one of whom was a confederate of the researcher. The confederate would then begin to act strange and Troy would observe the others' reaction. After completing it Troy put the work aside and never tried to publish it as a whole because it was not sufficiently grounded theoretically. However, in 1968 he published a study of an original laboratory experiment dealing with social deviance in the journal *Social Psychiatry*.[14] The conceptual part of this paper was taken from his PhD dissertation. The idea was to see what a naïve subject would do when confronted with six other members of the group who gave incorrect answers to a question posed by the researcher. Subjects either ignored the pressure from the group or responded with hostility to the group.

Despite his clear focus on mental illness, Troy found that many professors, like Kimball Young, very senior member of the faculty, wanted to talk
to him about black people, even though it was not his primary interest at the
time. This is the first example of Troy as an African American scholar being
forced to become a race expert.

POST-DOC

In 1962, as he was finishing his PhD at Northwestern, many of his friends
were getting grants from foundations such as the Ford Foundation or the
Rockefeller Foundation, which allowed them to teach either half-time or not
at all. He himself received a one-year post-doc from the Swedish government. He did research at Uppsala University in 1962–1963, writing about
control and deviance. His time in Sweden had several significant impacts on
his life. First, he learned that the Swedish upper-middle class was taxed a
great deal to cover various social welfare programs. Troy obviously thought
that the U.S. could learn a lot from Sweden's tax rates imposed on the
affluent. Second, he met Marie, who became his wife. In 1963 he and Marie
returned to California, where Troy had gotten a teaching position at University of California, Riverside.

Duster came to Riverside in 1963 partially because Aaron Cicourel had
become the department chair. He found his years in Riverside to be difficult.
He clashed with the conservative theorist Robert Nisbet and found Riverside
to be an unwelcoming community. His experience at Riverside was further
tainted by a severe illness that Marie experienced. She developed a 104-
degree fever. He took her to a private hospital, but the staff refused to treat
her because she had no health insurance. They were forced to go to the public
county hospital, where the medical staff at the public hospital misdiagnosed
her with disastrous results. Although her fever was broken, she had lifelong
medical issues as a result.[15] This experience led Troy to know the kind of
medical treatment the poor get in America, augmenting other experiences he
had as a child.

During his years at Riverside, 1963–1965, Troy began to publish in ear-
nest and began to give race a wider place in his studies. He published "The
Social Response to Abnormality"[16] (1963), and cowrote *Patterns of Minority
Relations* with Ray Mack (1964).[17] *Patterns of Minority Relations* argued
that race is a culturally created concept, not a biological category—a conception of race that continued throughout Troy Duster's career.

He later contributed a chapter to a book edited by Ray Mack (1968) about
his involvement with desegregation efforts of the Riverside schools after
arson destroyed one of Riverside's three minority elementary schools in
1965.[18] This incident was just one of many that caused Troy great frustration

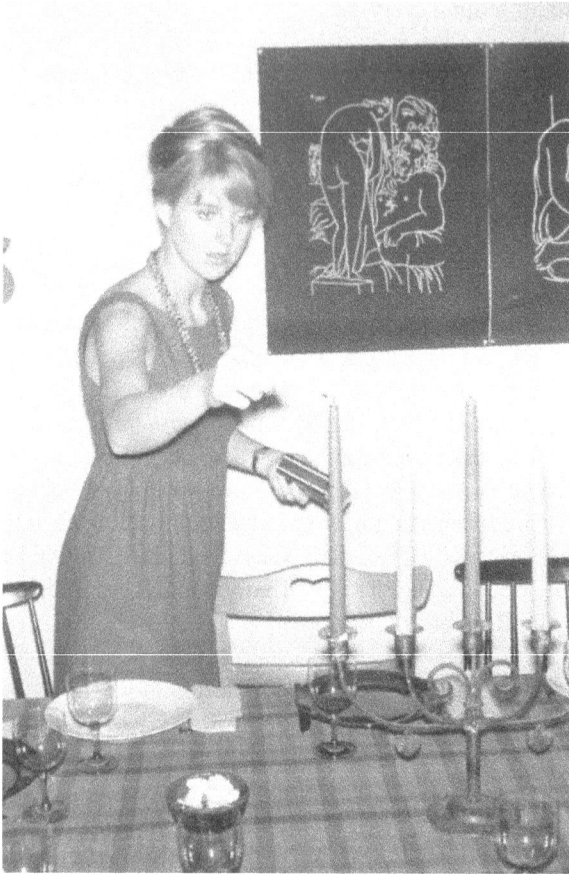

Figure 2.2. Marie in 1970.

in Riverside. As a black professor, anything Troy said made the local news. He had spoken out about U.S. civil rights and against the war in Vietnam. Accordingly, he often got hate mail and phone calls with death threats. Local realtors repeatedly told another African American professor at UC Riverside that they refused to deal with black clients. As a consequence, local black citizens were becoming increasingly militant and racial tensions were running relatively high. A hostile question regarding his being married to a white woman arose at the end of a speech on racial integration. Troy matched this hostility by asking his wife who was in the audience to stand, and he said sarcastically for the audience to "welcome her to the free world."[19]

With these frustrations piling up, Troy decided to leave Riverside, and in 1965 he did just that.

NOTES

1. Duster, "Oral History," 25.

2. Alondra Nelson, "Troy Duster: Interview," *Public Culture* 24 (2012): 283–302, 286–287.

3. Duster, "Oral History," 19.

4. Duster, "Oral History," 39.

5. Troy Duster, email to John Galliher, January 27, 2013.

6. Duster, "Oral History," 29.

7. Nelson, "Troy Duster: Interview."

8. Troy Duster, email to John Galliher, January 27, 2013.

9. Duster, "Oral History," 45.

10. Duster, "Oral History," 49.

11. Nathan Rosseau, *Self, Symbols and Society* (Lanham, MD: Rowman & Littlefield, 2002), 264.

12. Duster, "Oral History," 51.

13. Nelson, "Troy Duster: Interview."

14. Troy Duster, "Patterns of Deviant Reaction: Some Theoretical Issues," *Social Psychiatry* 3 (1968): 1–6.

15. Troy Duster, email to John Galliher, November 3, 2014.

16. Troy Duster, "The Social Response to Abnormality," *Research Reports in Sociology*, Uppsala, Sweden: Sociologiska Institutionen, Uppsala University, 1963.

17. Raymond Mack and Troy Duster, *Patterns of Minority Relations* (New York: Anti-Defamation League, 1964).

18. Troy Duster, "Violence and Civic Responsibility: Combinations of 'Fear' and 'Right,'" in Raymond Mack, ed., *Our Children's Burden: Studies in Desegregation in Nine American Cities* (New York: Vintage Books, 1968), 1–39.

19. Duster, "Oral History," 77.

Chapter Three

Professional Career

University of California, Berkeley

In the summer of 1965 Troy left Riverside and did a postdoc at Stockholm University from 1966 to 1967, where he did research on comparative controls of the universities in Sweden and the US. (He produced a report in 1968, "Aims and Controls of the Universities," for the Center for Research and Development in Higher Education in Berkeley, which had sponsored the postdoc position.) Upon returning to the US in 1967, he became an assistant research sociologist at the Center for Research and Development in Higher Education at Berkeley, a position he held until 1970, when he became associate professor. At Berkeley Troy often had an appointment in a research center or was the director of an institute where he had a half-time appointment, or served as department chair, so his teaching was only half time.

FIGURE 3.1. THE HISTORICAL, CULTURAL AND POLITICAL ENVIRONMENT OF BERKELEY SOCIOLOGY

The sociology department at Berkeley started with the establishment of the "social institutions" department in 1923. Berkeley had the taint of discrimination in its hiring practices, as did most universities. In 1946 Dorothy Swain Thomas was briefly considered for the position of chair of this department but was apparently rejected for this position because of blatant sexism.[1] And in the 1950s an African American named Blake Blackwell was considered for a position teaching sociology but was ultimately rejected because the wife of a senior faculty ember "didn't want a Darkie coming over for dinner."[2]

Figure 3.1. Troy as a young scholar at Berkeley.

The department made a giant leap forward when Herbert Blumer arrived in 1952 with the total support of then new Berkeley chancellor Clark Kerr. This time is sometimes referred to as the Golden Age of Sociology at Berkeley. Blumer was hired away from the University of Chicago in 1952 to come to Berkeley and build a new department of sociology.[3] Blumer had been forced to resign from Missouri University in the mid-1920s for his strident opposition of racism,[4] and if Chicago had not taken him in as an instructor and as a graduate student, he probably would not have been asked to lead the Berkeley department. If Blumer had not become the first chair of the department it probably would not have taken the direction that it did.

Blumer went on a hiring spree and recruited already established figures in the field—with something of a "star system," sometimes called the "satellite system."[5] His rationale was that he wanted a department in which the different perspectives and methods and theories could "have it out" in a continuous dialogue. It was Herb's lingering disappointment, and even depression, that each of the stars retreated to their own baronies (institutes) and never had the kind of intellectual exchanges (interactions as he would say) that he thought would benefit the discipline. In the early days of sociology at Berkeley there was no single, strong intellectual core, but critical sociology later came to the fore followed by public sociology, both of which had an adversarial relationship with society.[6]

Blumer hired notable sociologists including Seymour Martin Lipset, Reinhardt Bendix, Philip Selznick, Tamotsu Shibutani, Kingsley Davis, Nathan Glazer, William Kornhauser, and David Matza.[7] Claude Fischer joined the department in 1972 and referred to these senior people that Blumer recruited as "superstars from diverse fields including ethnographers, grand theorists and statistical types."[8] As a consequence of the faculty recruitment the department always attracted the best quality graduate students. The distinguished sociologists who Blumer hired ended up in their own research centers as was true in the department later. The Blumer system lasted approximately twenty-five years.[9]

TROY AT BERKELEY

In 1964 the student movement began, as did the Free Speech Movement. Eventually these movements split the department internally, but through it all graduate students were always protected, including Troy's many students whom he always protected.[10] In actual practice some faculty sided with the students, some were on the fence, and some were angrily opposed. Thus in the sociology department there was professional sociology that runs the risk of being trivial and remote, policy sociology that can become the prisoner of the world it studies, as well as critical sociology and public sociology. Many of these sociologists at Berkeley were people of the Left and were also interested in qualitative methods, as was Troy Duster. And Troy survived by navigating the conflicts in, and surrounding, the Berkeley department and stayed on from the 1960s to the late 1990s.

When Troy returned to Berkeley after his 1966–1967 postdoc at Stockholm University, everything regarding race had changed. Integration was no longer emphasized and now Black Power, Stokely Carmichael, H. Rap Brown, Bobby Seale and Eldridge Cleaver were center stage. Assimilation was now dead. The Black Panther Party had come into full flower. Initially the Party was solely devoted to stopping police brutality in Oakland. Later the Party moved to the Left by supporting revolution. Even later the Party supported school lunches and research into sickle cell anemia. Given these changes it was impossible for Troy to give his full support to the Party throughout these alternatives.[11]

Now Duster had moved to a permanent position at Berkeley. It was an unusual move in that he was heavily recruited by non-academics, including Huey Newton and the Black Panthers.[12] At the time Duster was seen by the Berkeley chancellor as needing police protection.

Troy noted that on the whole the department was not a supportive place. He opined: "the department, after all, was not a nurturing environment . . . the faculty are off in their different research institutes, and so literally you're lost if you come into the department . . . if you're first generation in college, as many of my students were."[13] Arlie Hochschild explained the situation as follows (2013): "The department had between 30–35 members and can best be described as a jungle. The University hired many gifted sociologists who were not good at community building. People like Kingsley Davis, Martin Lipset and Reinhardt Bendix."[14] Troy also recalled that Martin Lipset did not support the idea of affirmative action. But in the Berkeley department there was a "gang of four" who routinely voted with the graduate students on personnel matters: Troy, Bill Kornhauser, Robert Blauner, David Matza, later joined by Arlie Hochschild.[15] Matza noted that "for the first few years it was mostly a gang of four or five on matters such as department politics."[16]

When Troy's colleague, and another "gang of four" member, Robert Blauner (a one-time communist party member) and Troy decided to teach a theory course on Frantz Fanon, a black Marxist philosopher, some of their colleagues "went ballistic."[17] Generally faculty at Berkeley could teach whatever they wanted, but the graduate theory courses were different because a graduate theory course could substitute for the PhD exam in the area. "Until then the theory course was almost always on Weber, Durkheim, or Marx so including a black radical like Fanon was almost revolutionary." Blauner recalled that "it was my idea and I asked Troy to co-teach it for cover, for moral support."[18] Pedro Noguera noted in a 2013 interview that when he entered "the Berkeley graduate program the sociology department was very polarized."[19] Clearly the department's polarization is reflected in the response to the Fanon proposal. Troy noted that graduate students were incessantly subjected to "ceremonies of degradation."[20] And when graduate students of any ethnicity performed poorly they were expelled from the program. Troy admitted that several times he voted to drop students of all ethnicities from the program who didn't perform up to snuff.

The graduate students at Berkeley were "strongly phenomenological,"[21] like David Sudnow and his observational research on public defenders' decision making on reduced charges referred to as "Normal Crimes" published in *Social Problems* in 1965. "There were approximately an average of 200 graduate students during the period from 1970 to 2010. About 10 PhD students per year worked with Troy. Initially there were few people of color and women among these students but this percent grew rapidly because of Troy's influence."[22]

David Matza, who cowrote with Troy, noted:

> I haven't read Troy's *Legislation of Morality* (1970) since the 1970s and 1980s when I used to assign it in a Deviance course. He was one of those up and coming young sociologists who I heard about and read about even before we recruited him to Berkeley. He and I were part of the same sociological circles: Harold Garfinkel, Aaron Cicourel, Erving Goffman as well as Howard Becker, Sheldon Messinger, and Gresham Sykes, all a part of ethnomethodology, race relations and critical sociology. Troy's first book on *Legislation of Morality* immediately placed him in the front ranks of labeling theory, and integrated class and race factors.[23]

All of these sociologists produced qualitative research and were progressives, much like Troy. Troy demonstrated in his book on legislation that those who are poor and black are most easily labeled as drug-abusing criminals, using labeling theory ideas from Becker's book *Outsiders*.[24]

Troy had interactions with many influential colleagues over these years. Herbert Blumer, who was chair from 1952 to 1967, coined the term *symbolic interaction* to refer to a type of qualitative social psychology that emphasizes meaning to the actors involved. Erving Goffman shared an office with Troy during the first year after Troy arrived from Riverside in 1965. Goffman was at Berkeley from 1957 to 1968. Goffman used acting terms to refer to behavior that changed the way sociologists refer to and think about human interaction. In the 1960s Troy first met long-time friend Hardy Frye on a civil rights picket line.[25]

Robert Bellah joined the Berkeley faculty in 1967. Bellah wrote the influential book *Habits of the Heart* (1996), drawing on qualitative data to explain the rampant individualism in America. Arlie Hochschild joined this intellectual group as a faculty member in 1969, retired in 2006, and contributed the idea of *The Managed Heart* (published in 1983) and "commercialized feeling."

In the summer of 1965 Troy shared an office at Berkeley with Erving Goffman. Arthur Stinchcombe asked to see a draft of his book manuscript published in 1970, *Legislation of Morality*. This book covered the sociology of criminal law, especially the racism of drug laws. Troy found that in the past 150 years the problem of addiction had become "completely inverted."[26] In the late nineteenth century approximately two-thirds of white females were the primary users of heroin, while by 1925 users were primarily young, working-class, black men. As long as drug use was associated with prominent people it was tolerated by law enforcement. In the book Duster's "study of the California Rehabilitation Center covers the range of drugs used and more than a thousand individuals incarcerated there" and is used to provide an example of a total institution as described by Erving Goffman.[27]

After Stinchcombe read the manuscript of *Legislation of Morality,* he passed it around to the Berkeley faculty. It was on the basis of this manuscript that Troy achieved with tenure.

Duster's colleague David Matza sees *The Legislation of Morality* as singularly significant. Matza used this book in his deviance course during the 1970s and 1980s:

> His coverage of the range of effects, responses and treatments of illegal drugs from heroin, cocaine, LSD, ecstasy, and marijuana compared to the legal ones from morphine, methamphetamines and barbiturates and popular consumption of alcohol and tobacco are precise and correct in my opinion. Duster's book effectively challenges the prevailing view that the prohibition and criminalization is reasonable and correct policy.[28]

Figure 3.2. Barrows Hall at Berkeley. The fourth floor of Barrows Hall is the home of the sociology department.

Duster was elected president of the American Sociological Association (ASA) and a profile was written at the time about him by two friends that was published in the *ASA Newsletter*.[29] This essay noted that he had mentored many minority graduate students, over sixty-five at the time.

Figure 3.3. Photos of Troy taken in 1969 setting on steps and another in 1974 show Troy Duster in his early Berkeley years (Duster 2013a).

While at Berkeley, for over three decades from 1965 to 1999, Troy worked closely with university and student leaders during the Third World Strike (involving black and brown students) and the American Cultures requirement, of which he was the director. He was routinely involved with students in civil rights picketing[30] and became fast friends with minority students as a consequence. Discrimination continued to be an issue at Berkeley for years to come; in the 1990s many faculty left the department after Harry Edwards and Arlie Hochschild received tenure.[31]

Troy was the head of the campus Diversity Project head.[32] From 1976 to 1980 Troy "had an NIMH graduate student research training grant that funded about a dozen students, probably $130,000 per year. When Ronald Reagan came to power as U.S. president in 1980 this came to an end." The Reagan administration was attempting to cut the funding for the program and to medicalize it by having a physician on the staff of the Program.[33] This opposition occurred even though Berkeley was the only place producing many PhDs earned by people of color. Because the program was judged by the UC president to be very valuable "in training PhD students of color (Native-American, Asian-American, Latino, African- American—who routinely made up about half of the cohort),"[34] the UC president came up with the funding to replace the money was lost in 1980 because of Reagan. In addition to this support the local administration paid $90,000 per year to cover the costs of staffing the Institute. "Then there were always the research grants that faculty brought in" such as grants to Arlie Hochschild and David Matza. Such support varied from $250,000 to $500,000 per year. "Arlie received an NIMH grant to study her work in gender role shifts." "David Matza and David Wellman . . . got a huge grant to look at the long-shore [community] . . . with ethnographic field studies as the core."[35]

One of Troy's most important accomplishment's was his directorship of the Institute for the Study of Social Change—for twenty-one years, from about 1976 to 1997. The Institute suffered a crisis during the Reagan years of the 1980s. Troy noted that there was a paradigm shift among those running federal programs; they "said in effect, 'You want to fund real science? You [shouldn't] you fund that soft humanistic stuff.'"[36] However, Berkeley continued to support the Institute. Troy noted that after the Reagan-inspired cutbacks "ultimately I was able to get back $125,000 to $150,000 a year" from the campus as well as from the university administration. The support has its limits, however. The Institute is located in a bedraggled building about three blocks from campus. A long-term member of the sociology faculty, Arlie Hochschild, explains:

> Severe budget cuts have occurred at Berkeley and this has had a negative
> impact on the Institute but the Berkeley business school is going great guns.
> Correspondingly the change in name from the Institute for the Study of Social

Change to the Institute for the Study of Social Issues reflects a de-politization
of the Institute. While Troy was the Director of the Institute it served as a
protective shield for some faculty and graduate students. [37]

Eric Brown recalled that when he was a graduate student at Berkeley
(1980–1990) he routinely went to the Center to study. It served as a refuge
for him.

Troy always fought for rights at Berkeley for women and people of color.
Table 3.1 shows that over the years he chaired 46 PhD committees (the last
three students listed received a PhD from NYU. All the others received the
PhD from Berkeley, including those five earning the degree in 2000 or later.)
This service to Berkeley helps explain why Troy Duster was made a perma-
nent Chancellor's Professor there.

At least twenty-three of these students were women, four were Asian,
three were Jewish and the remainder were Hispanics or African Americans.
Troy explains these results as being a consequence demographic changes the
total graduate student population. "By the 1980s females were far and away
the majority of PhD students at Berkeley. Among white students the over-
whelming majority were Jewish."[38] Although Troy never chaired the committee of a white male Christian he did serve as a committee member (the

**Figure 3.4. The Institute for the Study of Social Change, later renamed the Insti-
tute for the Study of Social Issues.**

Table 3.1. Troy Duster's PhD Students

Name	Year of Completion
Judith Gaffin	1975
Carl Mack	1975
Gini Scott	1976
Leonarda Ybarra	1977
Geanne Pankey-Thompson	1978
Jerome Himmelstein	1979
Jack M. Bloom	1980
Jerrold Takahashi	1980
Steven Millner	1981
David Minkus	1981
Elizabeth Morgan	1981
John Dombrink	1981
Susan Takata	1983
Deborah Woo	1983
Annette Lareau	1984
Phillip B. Gonzales	1985
Elaine Draper	1985
Richard Morales	1985
Joan Fujimara	1986
Judy H. Rothschild	1986
Basil Browne	1988
Karen Hembry	1988
Eric Xavier	1988
Stephen Small	1989
Beverly John	1991
Howard Pinderhughes	1991
Oyeronke Oyewumi	1993
Larry Shinagawa	1994
Ann Ferguson	1995
Nadine Gartrell	1995
Jonathan Warren	1997
Rebecca King	1998
Ricky Blumenthal	1998

Pamela Perry	1998
Jiannbin Shiao	1998
Natasha Kraus	1999
Jacqueline Orr	1999
Eric Brown	1999
Kamau Birago	2000
Lorenza Hall	2001
Michael Hanson	2002
Naheem Islam	2002
Duana Fulwilley	2002
Alondra Nelson	2003
Shirley Sun	2005
Aaron Panofsky	2006
Ruha Benjamin	2008
Danielle Bessett	2009
Catherine Bliss	2009

second or third reader) for some these sociology graduate students. White male Christians Troy noted were typically either in the law school or the Berkeley business school. Broken down by decade the number of Berkeley students included 6 who completed their PhDs in the 1970s, 18 in the 1980s, 15 in the 1990s, decreasing to 5 in the 2000s, and finally 3 graduating from NYU during the period 1999–2012.

While very large, these numbers show nothing of the many students where Troy served as a mere reader of the students' MA and PhD committees. According to the University of California records the total sociology department committees is 91 as of 2014. Troy earned his salary as a UC Chancellor's Professor while at NYU since five UC students graduated while he was on the East Coast. The University of California records also show that Troy served on 35 committees as the "outside member" for students from other departments. The sum of Troy Duster's graduate committee responsibilities tops out at 126 or approximately 3 per year from 1970 to 2010. Suffice it to say that Troy was exceedingly busy with graduate teaching responsibilities.

Troy's research interests have shifted away from deviance to the sociology of science. In the 1990s the Ida B. Wells Memorial Foundation was established with a generous donation with Troy as the director. Each year a person is selected based on creative reporting of social justice for African Americans. This person is given $5,000 and a bust of Ida B. Wells. Also, beginning in the early 1970s Troy was the director of the NIMH training program for graduate students.

TEACHING AT BERKELEY

Throughout his career at both Berkeley and NYU Troy taught half of his courses at the undergraduate level and the other half at the graduate level (See Appendix A for syllabi). At the undergraduate level he taught Social Control and Deviance, Social Movements, and Introduction to Sociology. Graduate courses included Sociology of Science, Sociology of Law, Deviance and Control, Social Movements, and Field Research Methods.[39] Troy argued that if you are trying to conduct research on corporate America then problems of access must be a large part of what you are teaching. For over twenty years Troy taught courses on deviance and control.

In the 1960s the size of the black student body was 400 out of 20,000. But by 2003 there was a "critical mass" of black students at Berkeley so much so that "you could literally live your life at Berkeley and have only black friends."[40] Troy noted that when a black graduate student performed poorly you have to be willing to fail them but if there is any chance of success: "you've got to leave the door open for this person to come back, to take the exam again."[41] (175). An administrator in the sociology department named Carol Hatch was well liked by the graduate students because she had the ability to talk with the graduate students, could speak on their behalf and "she had an institutional memory of the old department."[42]

Two of Troy's colleagues in the sociology department Nathan Glazer and Martin Lipset were neoconservatives. Lipset disagreed with Troy regarding affirmative action. Yet Troy explained: "Quotas and inclusion basically are different. But Lipset said to me, 'Well I understand what you're saying, but we're going to part ways on this issue."[43] Bill Wilson has said that affirmative action is a failure because "it doesn't redress massive historical injustice; but Duster countered that it is not a "redress issue" but an "access issue."[44] In the mid-1990s at Berkeley Troy argued that affirmative action was merely a bandage to racial and ethnic stratification. The massive growth in the incarcerated black population can be explained by Sidney Willhelm's 1980 book *Who Needs the Negro*. For 250 years black labor was necessary, but in post-industrializing America black labor is no longer needed.

BERKELEY PUBLICATIONS

Troy's years at Berkeley were a richly productive time, and he published widely during his tenure there (see appendix B for a complete list of publications). In 1973 (*Science*) Troy published a book review of *Black Monday's*

Children. "The central thesis of this book ... is that black children in segregated Southern schools have significantly higher self-concepts than black children in desegregated schools ... A closer and yet bolder interpretation of the data of the study would have been a more illuminating strategy than this kind of reportage."[45] Troy had misgivings about this book, criticizing as it did racial integration. In 1976 (*The American Sociologist*) Troy wrote that the opponents of affirmative action have largely ignored the history that preceded this program.[46] There was a history of excluding blacks that existed both in labor unions and the business world. Troy also called attention to the social institutions that preserve the privilege and advantage of those on top.

In 1979 (*The American Sociologist*) Duster and two of his Berkeley colleagues (David Matza and David Wellman) criticized efforts to protect human subjects.[47] The problem with the law protecting human subjects is that it offers the most protection to those who need it the least—those on top. An example of this is demonstrated in HUD-sponsored research that found racial discrimination by realtors, where blacks were far less likely to be rented an apartment or sold a house. This type of research was already routinely prevented by government regulations. Thus in the final analysis realtors are protected at the expense of black citizens.

Next in 1981 (*Journal of Contemporary Studies*) Duster noted that a prominent author had argued against the minimum wage, affirmative action, policy efforts to desegregate schools and create schools with diverse social class backgrounds among students. The prominent author had used examples of Jews and Japanese to argue that special programs like desegregation and bilingual education are unnecessary. The difference is, according to Duster, that blacks and Hispanics are consistently poor.[48]

In 1987 Duster published an article ("Crime and Delinquency") where he penned the following: "at the same time that Black youth are typically seen as the most likely perpetrators of crime, Black youth are . . . also the group hardest hit by unemployment . . . It has become part of the conservative litany" to assert that only liberals still believed in the relationship between unemployment and crime. But Duster argued that this relationship in point of fact did exist.[49] In 1987 (*Society*) Duster wrote that while 28 percent of black Americans lived in poverty, this was true of only 7 percent of whites.[50] In 1995 (*The American Sociologist*) Duster showed that with the American war on drugs the nation has been building more prisons and imprisoning more than at any time in its history. It appears that racism is driving this repressive pattern. Nationwide 15–20 percent of drug users are black but half to two-thirds of those arrested for drug offenses are black.[51]

In a 1995 essay (*Crossroads*) Duster hinted at what would become a decade later a primary concern—that there remained a search for biological causes of deviant behavior including homelessness, violence, and crime.[52] Society seems inevitably concerned with virtue on the top but trouble on the bottom. Herbert Spencer developed social Darwinism and the notion of the survival of the fittest. Spencer noted that black American children could not keep up with whites because of blacks' genetic limitations. This ideology led to the 1920s racist immigration laws and to involuntary sterilization laws of the 1930s and 1940s. These immigration laws contributed to the exclusion of Jews during the Holocaust.

In 1996 (*Representations*) Duster wrote that California from the 1970s to the 1990s had become much more diverse with whites composing barely a majority of the state's population.[53] On the other hand African Americans made up only 7 percent of the total population of California compared to 12 percent nationally. Troy said that he wrote this essay to demonstrate the changing demographic environment existing for all UC campuses. He did this in response to the passage in California of Prop 209, which constitutionally abandoned affirmative action at Berkeley and all other state agencies.[54] Without affirmative action blacks would virtually disappear from UC Berkeley. In a similar way in a 1996 article (*Ethics and Policy*) Duster argued that in accessing affirmative action policies that allow African Americans to be given priority for admission to UC Berkeley over whites, it is important to consider the context to make a sensible appraisal of fairness. Whites in the U.S. have for many decades been free to accumulate wealth so that currently the mean worth of the white family is approximately four times that of the black family. Thus it does not make sense to say now "Let's abandon any attempts to redress the previous [outcome of the system and] let's use only individual merit."[55]

In a 1971 essay Duster mentions the Berkeley conflict over the issue of autonomy of black studies programs.[56] In a 1985 essay Duster wrote that in 1969 the unemployment rate for black youth ages 16–19 was 12.1 percent but by 1983 it was a whopping 48.3 percent.[57] Since 1979 there have been thousands of plant closings around big cities where the bulk of blacks reside. To take up the slack a flourishing heroine trade is also concentrated in these areas. A 1997 essay further examines how the war on drugs has contributed to racial injustice.[58] In 1954 black and white unemployment were approximately equal but by 1984 the unemployment rate by blacks had quadrupled while the white rate had remained approximately the same. And according to the U.S. government statistics blacks comprised 15–20 percent of drug users but 66 percent of those arrested for drug offenses. Just part of this difference can be accounted for by the fact that higher-level dealers (who are often white) can bargain more with law enforcement because they know more about the business than others and can trade information for their freedom. The shift from an industrial to a service economy has hurt blacks more than whites; for example many crack dealers earlier had factory jobs.

Another book chapter published in 1993 deals with diversity at the University of California at Berkeley.[59] Troy wrote that the debate about multiculturalism was increasingly mean spirited. It is worth noting that Hillel and the Newman Center were outgrowths of discrimination against Jews and Catholics on campus. In 1960 Berkeley was made up of 90 percent white students while in 1993 it was approximately 45 percent, with Asians being the dominant group, in terms of performance. A two-year study of student life and diversity at Berkeley found 70 percent of all Berkeley undergraduate students wanted to meet more students from different ethnic backgrounds. But 72 percent of black students were interested in programs to promote racial understanding while only a minority of white students were interested. This difference may be a source of a continuing conflict at Berkeley.

In 1984 Duster and Garrett wrote, "Genes almost always determine sex and race, but circumstance will always determine which is more important in a struggle for resources and power."[60] In the first chapter of this book Duster noted that in the late nineteenth-century scholars pointed to biological causes of crime.[61] Duster also observed that although sickle cell anemia was recognized seventy years ago it was slow to attract attention. Attention should be given to where biological knowledge is stressed. In 1990 Duster wrote a book (*Backdoor to Eugenics*) where he observed that eugenics between 1925 and 1950 shifted away from feeble-minded Jews to lower IQs among blacks.[62] To demonstrate that it is still timely this book was used in a 2013 *American Sociological Review* article[63] where Duster's ideas were tested and these results suggest an unintended consequence of the genomic revolution may be the reinvigoration of age-old faith in essential racial differences and thus confirms what Duster argued in *Backdoor to Eugenics*.

A book chapter Troy published in 1971 provides an early intellectual baseline.[64] It deals with legal control of different types of drugs in the U.S. and the irrationality of these laws with nary a mention of race, racism, or genetics. In 1987 (*The American Sociologist*) Duster described the Berkeley sociology graduate program.[65] This program creates a large number of dissertations that are "sole-authored independent books and monographs" as opposed to a more formulaic program where students work as an apprentice with a senior scholar. Troy himself was nearly always ready to direct a minority student's dissertation. The Berkeley program was a double-edged sword and was anomic, allowing as it did some failures. These two articles say nothing explicitly about race.

TROY'S PERSONAL LIFE AT BERKELEY

Levine and Reinarman (2004) noted that through the years Troy kept a brown-shingle home in Berkeley (approximately one mile south of campus) where he built on a kitchen that allowed him to prepare gourmet meals to entertain his friends; he also became a ceramic artist and installed a kiln in his garage.[66] Troy purchased the home in 1973 for $46,000 and according to a 2013 electronic realty ad was valued at $1,200,000. According to Troy this can be seen as a "brilliant investment signaling, among other things, how smart one is to be born at the right time, in the right place."[67] The house is approximately one mile from campus and about a block and a half from many small restaurants, bars, a very small movie theater, and other businesses, businesses all frequented primarily by UC Berkeley students.

Troy Duster also had a passion for music, playing the cello. He says that he collected between four and five thousand, mainly classical, albums (54). Troy elaborated on his musical background: "I actually took cello lessons when I was studying for my PhD but never progressed to a skill level to the point where I could play with a group. My cello is somewhere in the attic, and I have not touched it in years. I also played around with the guitar [in a heartfelt fashion a 1970 photo; see figure 3.9], especially in the period in the 60s and 70s when people would bring guitars to parties and sit around and sing blues and folk songs. [Otherwise] my taste in music is ecumenical"— from classical to jazz and gospel.[68]

Figure 3.5. A photo provided by Troy (Duster 2013c) showing his ivy-covered house is seen below. Just south of Troy's home is a double wide trailer. Any where besides Berkeley this area would qualify as an upper-working-class neighborhood. Photo courtesy of Troy Duster.

Figure 3.6. An undated photo of Troy from friend Russ Ellis (Duster 2013d), apparently with pots and pans hanging from the wall in the kitchen of his Berkeley home, suggests the significance of the room for him.

Figure 3.7. The spirit of Troy Duster is also captured in one of his favorite Berkeley places, the city Rose Garden (Duster 2013c) that has approximately 250 rose varieties and stunning views of the San Francisco Bay and the Golden Gate Bridge.

Figure 3.8. The Rose Garden at Berkeley (Duster 2013c).

Figure 3.9. Troy in 1970 (Duster 2013c).

Figure 3.10. The entrance to Chez Panisse. Troy published a paper with owner Alice Water regarding the relationship between public education, growing one's own food, and healthy eating.

Figure 3.9. One of Troy's favorite Berkeley restaurants is the Chez Panisse Café, and in recent years Troy has been on the Board of Directors of the Chez Panisse Foundation, recently renamed the Edible Schoolyard Project.[69] Early in his association with Alice Waters, director of the Chez Panisse Foundation, Troy prepared a meal for her that was an elaborate Japanese dinner that showed off his skills as a gourmet chef featuring fresh eel. Troy is a connoisseur of fine wines and classical music and a fine potter. He is also an expert photographer. In short, according to his friend Thelton Henderson Troy is a renaissance man.[70] Involvement in this project is consistent with Troy advocating a close relationship between public education, growing one's own food, and healthy eating. Indeed, in 2006 Troy published a paper with Alice Waters in *Liberal Education* on this topic.[71]

Troy's marriage to Marie dissolved in 1972 after ten years. She just didn't fit in at Berkeley and desperately wanted to go back to Sweden. Troy held a going-away party for her. She was remarried in Sweden and upon a return visit some years later Troy threw another dinner for her inviting all their old friends to see her again (Henderson 2013).

NOTES

1. Michael Burawoy and Jonathan VanAntwerpen, *Berkeley Sociology: Past, Present and Future*, unpublished manuscript, November 2001.
2. David Minkus, interview with Eric Brown, September 16, 2013.
3. Troy Duster, email to John Galliher, May 8, 2014.

4. David Patrick Keys and John F. Galliher, *Confronting the Drug Control Establishment: Alfred Lindesmith as a Public Intellectual* (Albany: SUNY Press, 2000).

5. Troy Duster, email to John Galliher, May 18, 2014.

6. Burawoy and VanAntwerpen, *Berkeley Sociology.*

7. Burawoy and VanAntwerpen, *Berkeley Sociology.*

8. Claude Fischer, telephone interview with John Galliher, June 6, 2014.

9. Troy Duster, email to John Galliher, May 18, 2014.

10. Claude Fischer, telephone interview with John Galliher, June 6, 2014.

11. Troy Duster, email to John Galliher, May 28, 2014.

12. Alondra Nelson, "Troy Duster: Interview," *Public Culture* 24 (2012): 283–302.

13. Troy Duster, "An Oral History with Troy Duster," interview conducted by Richard Cándida Smith and Nadine Wilmot, 2002–2003, Regional Oral History Office, The Bancroft Library, University of California, Berkeley, 2012, 178.

14. Arlie Hochschild, phone interview with John Galliher, June 21, 2013.

15. Duster, "An Oral History," 138.

16. David Matza, email to John Galliher. April 18, 2013.

17. Duster, "Oral History," 112.

18. Robert Blauner, email to John Galliher, April 21, 2013.

19. Pedro Noguera, telehpone interview with John Galliher, April 13, 2013.

20. Duster, "Oral History," 144.

21. Duster, "Oral History," 121.

22. Arlie Hochschild, phone interview with John Galliher, June 21, 2013.

23. David Matza, email to John Galliher, April 12, 2013.

24. Howard S. Becker, *Outsiders* (New York: Free Press, 1963).

25. Hardy Frye, interview by Eric Brown, July 7, 2013.

26. Nelson, "Troy Duster," 296.

27. Erving Goffman, *Asylums: Essays on the Social Situation of Mental Patients and Other Inmates* (New York: McGraw-Hill, 1961).

28. David Matza, email to John Galliher, April 12, 2013.

29. Harry Levine and Craig Reinarman, "Profile of the ASA President, Troy Duster: A Biography in History," *ASA Footnotes*, September/October 2004.

30. Hardy Frye, interview by Eric Brown, July 7, 2013.

31. Troy Duster, email to John Galliher, June 8, 2013.

32. Troy Duster and Karen Garrett, eds., "Introduction," in *Cultural Perspectives on Biological Knowledge*, ed. Troy Duster and Karen Garrett, vii–xiv (Norwood, NJ: Ablex, 1984), vii.

33. Nelson, "Troy Duster," 297.

34. Troy Duster, email to John Galliher, June 8, 2013.

35. Duster, "Oral History," 148.

36. Duster, "Oral History," 167.

37. Arlie Hochschild, phone interview with John Galliher, June 21, 2013.

38. Troy Duster, email to John Galliher, December 5, 2013.

39. Troy Duster, email to John Galliher, January 27, 2013.

40. Duster, "Oral History," 283.

41. Duster, "Oral History," 175.

42. Duster, "Oral History," 139.

43. Duster, "Oral History," 114.

44. Duster, "Oral History," 44.

45. Troy Duster, "Book Review: School Desegregation as a Psychological Factor," *Science* 181 (1973): 46–47.

46. Troy Duster, "The Structure of Privilege and Its Universe of Discourse," *The American Sociologist* 11 (1976): 73–78.

47. Troy Duster, David Matza, and David Wellman, "Field Work and the Protection of Human Subjects," *The American Sociologist* 14 (August 1979): 136–142.

48. Troy Duster, "The Ideological Frame of 'Benign Neglect,'" *Journal of Contemporary Studies* (Winter 1981): 81–90.

49. Troy Duster, "Youth Unemployment, and the Black Urban Underclass," *Crime and Delinquency* 33 (April 1987): 300–316.

50. Troy Duster, "Purpose and Bias," *Society* (January/February 1987): 8–12.

51. Troy Duster, "The New Crisis of Legitimacy in Controls, Prisons, and Legal Structures," *The American Sociologist* (Spring 1995): 20–29.

52. Troy Duster, "The Hidden History of 'Scientific' Racism," *Crossroads*, February 1995, 14–19.

53. Troy Duster, "Individual Fairness, Group Preferences, and the California Strategy," *Representations*, 1996, 41–58.

54. Troy Duster, email to John Galliher, August 29, 2014.

55. Troy Duster, "Public Forum: Affirmative Action: It's Just Not Fair," *Ethics and Policy* (Winter 1996): 2–7.

56. Troy Duster, "The Third World College and the Colonial Analogy," in *The University Crisis Reader: The Liberal University Under Attack*, vol. 1, ed. Emmanuel Wallerstein and Paul Starr, 240–243 (New York: Random House, 1971).

57. Troy Duster, "Social Implications of the 'New' Black Urban Underclass," *Poverty with a Human Face: Poverty, Justice and Equality in the Contemporary United States*, ed. Clayborne Carson and Mark McLeod, 47–55 (San Francisco: Public Media Center, 1985).

58. Troy Duster, "Pattern, Purpose and Race in the Drug War: The Crisis of Credibility in Criminal Justice," in *Crack in America: Demon Drugs and Social Justice*, ed. Craig Reinarman and Harry G. Levine, 260–287 (Berkeley: University of California Press, 1997).

59. Troy Duster, "The Diversity of California at Berkeley: An Emerging Reformulation of 'Competence' in an Increasingly Multicultural World," in *Beyond a Dream Deferred: Multicultural Education and the Politics of Excellence*, ed. Becky W. Thompson and Sangeeta Tyagi, 231–255 (Minneapolis: University of Minnesota Press, 1993).

60. Duster and Garrett, "Introduction," vii.

61. Troy Duster, chapter 1 in *Cultural Perspectives on Biological Knowledge*, ed. Troy Duster and Karen Garrett, 1–40 (Norwood, NJ: Ablex, 1984).

62. Troy Duster, *Backdoor to Eugenics* (New York: Routledge, 1990).

63. Jo C. Phelan, Bruce C. Link, and Naumi M. Freeman, "The Genomic Revolution and Beliefs about Differences," *American Sociological Review* 78, no. 1 (February 2013): 1–25.

64. Troy Duster, "Drugs and Drug Control," in *Crime and Justice in American Society*, ed. Jack D. Douglas, 195–235 (New York: Bobbs-Merrill, 1971).

65. Troy Duster, "Graduate Education at Berkeley," *The American Sociologist* (Spring 1987): 83–86.

66. Levine and Reinarman, "Profile of the ASA President, Troy Duster."

67. Troy Duster, email to John Galliher, January 15, 2015.

68. Troy Duster, email to John Galliher, January 26, 2013.

69. Troy Duster, email to John Galliher, March 15, 2013.

70. Thelton Henderson, interview by Eric Brown, July 19, 2013.

71. Troy Duster and Alice Waters, "Engaged in Learning Across the Curriculum," *Liberal Education* (Spring 2006): 42–47.

Chapter Four

Internal Dynamics of the Berkeley Sociology Department

AFFIRMATIVE ACTION AND BLACK STUDIES AT BERKELEY

Berkeley was later in establishing a sociology department than other elite institutions. However, once the department was founded, it quickly moved ahead of Harvard and Chicago, which were each divided by conflict. Marxist sociology emerged at Berkeley, but the students in the Free Speech Movement divided the sociology faculty. On top of this Eldridge Cleaver in 1968 was invited by Troy Duster and others in the department to give a new course on campus. Governor Reagan demanded that it should carry no credit. In the mid- to late 1960s many were leaving the department to avoid the conflict: Seymour Martin Lipset for Harvard in 1965, Nathan Glazer also to Harvard in 1969, and Erving Goffman to Pennsylvania in 1968. But by the mid-1970s the department was rebuilding and including a more diverse of faculty and students, including people of color and women.[1]

Troy observed that students of color found special difficulties in graduate school because they are often the first people in their families to attend college, much less graduate school. On a related issue the black studies department wanted autonomy, but the university administration said that they couldn't have autonomy. In the late 1960s Chancellor Roger Heynes said that he could not permit an all-black black studies program, even though the political science department at that time was all white. According to Troy "an all white political science department is simply a *fait accompli* because of the forces of history."[2] At the time the Berkeley political science department didn't have a course on urban politics or black mayors even though most of the largest American cities had black mayors. With the Reagan revolution, the victory of conservative House Speaker Gingrich, and Bill Clinton moving

35

to the center, the war on welfare was completed and "won by those who said 'Get off welfare, get on your own feet, get a job.'"[3]

At one point 34 percent of Asians applicants were eligible for admittance into Berkeley, 15 percent of whites and 4 to 5 percent of blacks and Latinos.[4] Asians now represent 12 percent of the state's population, blacks only 7 percent. Yet even with the depressing numbers of Berkeley-eligible, the political right routinely criticizes the poor success rate for blacks and Latinos.[5] George Napper was a Berkeley graduate student in criminology whose dissertation became a book titled *Blacker Than Thou: The Struggle for Campus Unity;*[6] he was also Troy's friend and was trusted by the other graduate students. Napper became police chief of Atlanta and then chief and commissioner of public safety in New York City.

Troy Duster also worked with Asian, black, and Hispanic graduate students at Berkeley. Jere Takahashi was a Japanese American in the Asian American studies program who earned a BA, MA and PhD at Berkeley:

> I began in 1971 and took seminars from Troy since I was involved in the NIMH traineeship that Troy directed [later Troy was the director of the Institute for the Study of Social Change[, although I actually began graduate school to study with Herbert Blumer to become a symbolic interactionist and an expert on race and ethnicity. Troy was a wonderful faculty member and advisor who could get to the core of an issue. At one point as a graduate student I was bogged down and Troy gave me advice that helped me get through the program. Unlike some faculty at Berkeley Troy did not seek the limelight. I was a frequent visitor at his house for a meal. Thelton Henderson was a recently retired federal judge who was also one of his friends who he frequently entertained at his house.[7]

Stephen Small is a black man in the Berkeley African American studies department. He commented on his experience with Troy as well:

> I studied with Troy as a graduate student in sociology from 1984 to 1989. During this time he was also director of the Institute for the Study of Social Change. He was especially good at extending knowledge across the nation and even the world. He was very generous with his time and highly responsive and always able to provide the larger context for my research on the Caribbean. As director of the Institute he taught students about field research methods and in this capacity he always had visitors to campus who were well-known. He always asked me if I had time to meet them—people like Aaron Cicourel. Eventually in 1994 I became his colleague and I was chair of my own department in 2002–2004.[8]

Pedro Noguera is an Hispanic man. He recalled:

> I began the PhD program at Berkeley in 1980. Although he was a mentor he did not chair my committee. I took a graduate Sociology of Science course

from him and later was a TA for him in his undergraduate Deviance course. I was supported for a time by a grant from the Institute for the Study of Social Change that Troy headed. As a mentor he would just let you do what you wanted to do and would merely show you how to do it.

When I arrived at Berkeley the sociology department was very polarized. Even though Troy was definitely a progressive he was still very respected by all faculty in the department. It's hard for me to know the basis of all the divisions since I was a graduate student and not privy to all the backroom conversations. My sense is that the divisions were left/right ideological differences, compounded by fierce battles over tenure decisions. What I remember being told by more advanced doctoral students is that you had to choose your committee carefully because if you ended up with people from opposing factions on your committee things might not go so well.[9]

Pedro also remembered that

Troy was also a political advisor to me. I was the first African American to be elected president of the student body and I gained a lot from his input. Berkeley Chancellor Heymans also respected him. Troy was also quite involved politically in the community of Berkeley. After he retired from Berkeley I replaced him as the director of the Institute for the Study of Social Change and I am now at NYU.

The great respect that Troy commanded in the sociology department at Berkeley is confirmed by Bob Blauner's decision to ask Troy to co-teach the graduate theory seminar on Franz Fanon to provide the enterprise with intellectual cover.

TROY DUSTER AND WOMEN AT BERKELEY

Although he was not an opponent of feminists Troy recalled that "I was hardly part of the vanguard of feminist thought, feminist work."[10] Nonetheless, Troy had no difficulty in relating to women who were graduate students. Duana Fullwiley from Stanford University worked with Troy on an undergraduate honors thesis at Berkeley where he directed readings for her in 1993 and later a PhD dissertation. In 1995 she also worked with him as a teaching fellow for a class titled Deviance and Social Control. "He was a key player in getting scientists interested in genetic issues around race and difference."[11]

Joan Fijumira from the University of Wisconsin recalled:

I entered the graduate program at Berkeley in 1978. I was initially interested in symbolic interaction and medical sociology; thus my first two advisors were Howie Becker, who has a flat in San Francisco, and Anselm Strauss at the University of California-San Francisco. After that I became interested in the physical sciences and cells. In 1980 I pursued the sociology of science in the natural sciences and fortunately in the 70s there was a renewed interest in the topic. Troy always let me do what I wanted to do. He recruited a geneticist for my graduate committee who worked well with social scientists. Troy was director of the Institute for the Study of Social Change and in that capacity gave me a small amount of money to begin a group on women of color. Troy told me, 'Remember that not every woman of color will be your friend.' Troy continues to assist me. In 2004 I organized a symposium on race and science and he, of course, participated. Earlier in the year (2013) there was a convention in Singapore on genetics and Troy was there. I've just completed an issue of *Social Studies of Science* and Troy and I were coeditors of the special issue. [12]

COLLEAGUES, FRIENDS AND OTHERS

Professor Charis Thompson in the department of women and gender studies has a very high opinion of Troy Duster: "What's not to love about him as a colleague?"[13] Later Thompson recalled that she cochaired a PhD dissertation committee with Troy and that "he stands out for his leadership in all things related to genes, race, and society."[14] Arlie Hochschild said that she was a longtime friend and admirer of Troy's:

Figure 4.1. Photo taken in the late 1970s show Troy as a mature scholar.

Figure 4.2. Photo taken in the late 1970s show Troy as a mature scholar. Courtesy of Russell Ellis.

> You went to him when you were in trouble. He is not a racist, he says, "because one of his grandfathers was white." In the 1960s there was the women's movement, the civil rights movement, the anti-war movement and the Free Speech Movement. Troy held the gang of five together even though the rest of the department didn't like it. In fact Harold Wilensky was so horrified that he transferred to political science. [15]

Thelton remembered that he was a varsity track athlete at UCLA and originally met Troy and his wife Marie in the early to mid-1960s at the dinner party at the home of Russ Ellis, who along with Troy was a professor at UC Riverside.[16] At the time Thelton was an attorney practicing in the Bay area. Sociologist Aaron Cicourel, the Riverside sociology department chair, was also at the dinner party. (Thelton has since been appointed a federal district trial judge). Shortly after the Riverside dinner party and unknown to Thelton, Troy was interviewed for a job at Berkeley and by chance Thelton bumped into him as Troy was walking down Telegraph Street. Since money was very tight at the university Troy and his wife stayed at Thelton's house during the interview. "Troy has an amazing social life but still manages to publish frequently. My guess is that he manages to get by with three hours' sleep. As it happens, Russ, Troy, and I have similar brown-shingled houses within five blocks of one another in Berkeley."[17]

Figure 4.3. Photo taken in the late 1970s show Troy as a mature scholar. Courtesy of Troy Duster.

THE GANG OF FOUR, FIVE, OR MORE

According to David Matza Troy was an integral part of the gang of five. Matza noted: "Russ Ellis is at Left End, Troy is Left Tackle, Bob Blauner is at Right Guard, Henry Miller is at Right End, and Matza is the Quarterback. This gang had no Center and maybe that is why the gang kept changing and suffered frequent if not chronic conflicts." Troy met Russ Ellis when they were both students at UCLA and Russell was an undergraduate. And it was through Russell Ellis that Thelton Henderson met Troy.[18] In a later message Matza said he could not recount these conflicts because they were too "petty and painful to recollect. It was sort of ideological, sort of who was working closely with whom and who was getting funded. Typically academic."[19] Given these divisions it is even more impressive that Troy was so productive during the years at UC Berkeley. We know that the department was not totally in his camp, but even his friends were not always supportive.

Figure 4.4. Troy with Russ Ellis on the left and California federal district trial judge Thelton Henderson center.

DEPARTMENT LEADERSHIP AT BERKELEY

Troy became department chair in 1985. From his earliest days at Berkeley Troy has had direct access to the chancellor's office. After he refused to accept the position of department chair in 1982 Troy was offered it again in 1985. This time he accepted the position since the chancellor gave $25,000 to the department. "My colleagues thought I was a miracle worker since as a consequence of taking the position we were able to hire two women."[20]

In 1979 he had already been appointed director of the Institute for the Study of Social Change, referring to his appointment in the Institute as his "barony."[21] In 1973 he received federal money and became the director of the NIMH training program for graduate students. Later Troy became director of American cultures studies as well. In this capacity he dealt directly with the chancellor, and this created bureaucratic jealousy and pettiness since he was going around the chain of command (there were several official command positions between Troy and the chancellor). And "I found myself routinely on the side of feminists," likely also generating ill feelings. "At one point the department was subject to an external review and determined that this was not a place for quality theoretical work. So I went uncharacteristically ballistic."

Figure 4.5. The Gang of Five. A photo from the mid-1970s shows progressive friends and colleagues at the beach. Troy is at the rear right drinking from a bottle and David Matza is shown holding a football (2013). The front row from left to right includes: Henry Miller, Bob Blauner and Russ Ellis.

In 2000 the National Institute of Health (NIH) was mandated by Congress to see what caused different rates of disease among various ethnic and racial groups. For example, black males have twice the rate of prostate cancer as white males and "sickle-cell had become a racialized disease."[22] The Human Genome Project, which Troy directed at Berkeley, was funded heavily on fourteen different campuses. He was a member of the national budget council of this project and for a time chaired the ethical and social issues panel. For the first decade of the project it was routinely claimed that all people were alike, but later the project emphasized differences. Supreme Court Justice Clarence Thomas and Ward Connerly argue that consideration of race and ethnicity should be junked.

Chancellor Mike Heymans diverted some Asian and white students to other UC campuses to make way for Latino and African American students at Berkeley. This policy encouraged George Will, Dinesh D'Souza, Thomas Sewell, and Linda Chavez to criticize it. While affirmative action did not solve the problem of poverty in America, criticism of it was sometimes "duplicitous and intended to undermine what affirmative action has accomplished."[23]

CLOSING OF THE BERKELEY SCHOOL OF CRIMINOLOGY

According to Matza an important part of this story of campus diversity involves the sensational closing of the School of Criminology at Berkeley in 1976. At this time criminology was in its infancy and the Berkeley program was among the best, if not the best, in the area. Its closing is typically seen as the result of the dictates of the far-right California governor Ronald Reagan, who led the state from 1967 to 1975. But that is only part of the story. In 1960 Joseph Lohman was hired to become the new dean of the school and as a consequence it assumed a more liberal and sophisticated character.[24] Lohman hired several prominent but aging criminologists to aid the school in achieving new power. When the dean died suddenly in 1968 it created a power vacuum that allowed even more democratic forms of governance to emerge. Yet the progress was marred by the fact that progressive whites did not give sufficient emphasis to the fight against racism.

David Matza reports that the school was weakened by faculty in-fighting.[25] There was a rift between radical faculty Paul Takagi and Tony Platt, who had sided with student strikers, and other, more established faculty including Sheldon Messinger. Matza recalled that this split alienated him (as well as Troy Duster) since he could be friendly with either side. Both sides however became enemies of the university administration due to the chronic conflict, and thus the school became an easy target for expulsion. It was closed in 1976.

NOTES

1. Michael Burawoy and Jonathan VanAntwerpen, *Berkeley Sociology: Past, Present and Future*, unpublished manuscript, November 2001.
2. Troy Duster, "An Oral History with Troy Duster," interview conducted by Richard Cándida Smith and Nadine Wilmot, 2002–2003, Regional Oral History Office, The Bancroft Library, University of California, Berkeley, 2012, 104.
3. Duster, "Oral History," 229.
4. Duster, "Oral History," 248.
5. Duster, "Oral History," 250.
6. George Napper, *Blacker Than Thou: The Struggle for Campus Unity* (Grand Rapids, MI: Eerdmans, 1973).
7. Jere Takahashi, phone interview with John Galliher, February 4, 2013.
8. Stephen Small, phone interview with John Galliher, February 13, 2013.
9. Pedro Noguera, phone interview with John Galliher, February 20, 2013, and email to John Galliher, May 12, 2013.
10. Duster, "Oral History," 173.
11. Duana Fullwiley, email to John Galliher, January 22, 2013
12. Joan Fijumira, phone interview with John Galliher, April 4, 2013.
13. Charis Thompson, interview with John Galliher, March 15, 2013.
14. Charis Thompson, interview with John Galliher, May 23, 2013.
15. Arlie Hochschild, phone interview with John Galliher, June 21, 2013.
16. Thelton Henderson, interview with Eric Brown, July 13, 2013.
17. Thelton Henderson, email to John Galliher, March 13, 2013.

18. Thelton Henderson, phone interview with John Galliher, April 30, 2013.

19. David Matza, email to John Galliher, April 13, 2013.

20. Troy Duster, email to John Galliher, May 28, 2014.

21. Duster, "Oral History," 145.

22. Duster, "Oral History," 188.

23. Duster, "Oral History," 259.

24. Tony Platt, Greg Shank, Paul Takagi, and Herman Schwendinger, "Editorial: Berkeley School of Criminology, 1950–1976," *Social Justice* (1976).

25. David Matza, email to John Galliher, April 13, 2013.

Chapter Five

Professional Career

New York University

In 1999, Troy made a major change in his life. He decided to leave Berkeley, although Chancellor Berdahl tried hard to convince him to stay. Troy informed him of how pivotal the American Cultures Center was to diversity on campus. The chancellor promised to invest in the center, even though the climate immediately following the passage of Prop 209 (prohibiting preference for minorities) changed student demographics overnight.

Troy moved to New York and began teaching at New York University. Troy spoke about the differences between NYU and Berkeley:

> I had to learn the differences between a public and private university. NYU is like a barony in that administrators can create a new center to attract a faculty member that they want but a new dean can simply close the center once he takes over. This fast action simply could not happen at Berkeley. Also at Berkeley the administration rarely challenged faculty governance—only once I can think of. It was in the case of the promotion of Harry Edwards. But the administration at a private institution has a lot of power. During my first two years at NYU I was learning the difference. Also, in NYC the faculty has many other things to call for their attention, such as the ballet, symphonies, opera, and of course the theatre; and so if university faculty meeting is called and only 20 people show up the administration knows it can ignore the faculty.
>
> During the next phase at NYU I got a Ford Foundation grant to pull people together every two to three2– weeks who were interested in science and society—people from the Graduate Center, Queens, the New School, and Columbia. Also at this point the Institute for the Production of Knowledge made possible a lot of co-teaching across departments. At Berkeley it was much more difficult to teach across departments. By this time I began to get more graduate students to work with.[1]

In 1999 UC Chancellor Berdahl gave Troy a permanent appointment as a Chancellor's Professor even while he was at NYU. This appointment allowed him to return to Berkeley occasionally to teach in the graduate program.[2] He was incredibly productive during his NYU years: approximately half of Duster's articles were published during the thirteen years (2000–2012) that he was at NYU. His NYU colleague and friend Craig Calhoun spoke of his work:

> Much of his best work was done at Berkeley of course, including almost all that on crime, deviance, and legislating morality. But he also became deeply involved in faculty politics and center administration. He arrived at NYU with fewer administrative obligations and a new set of stimulating colleagues focused on the sociology of knowledge and bioscience. He was also fresh from his service on the Human Genome Project's committee on social and ethical implications. This gave him new ideas and data on which to work—and some sense of public policy urgency.[3]

This new interest in bioscience is evident in his publications, which transition from an earlier concern with racism to a general (but not total) emphasis on how racism is expressed through the use of genetics. In 2001 in *The Chronicle of Higher Education* Duster wrote that some of those on the political left have argued that class is more significant than race in determining behavior and more recently those on the right have clamored for an end to affirmative action since they argue that we live in a postracial society.[4] In several publications in the 2000s, Troy disputed this. He argued that although all races share 99.9 percent of their DNA, race is still a compelling, socially constructed issue.

Troy demonstrated the impact of the social construction of race in several ways.[5] For example, even though DNA samples show that people are 99.9% alike, DNA is still used to identify the race of criminal suspects. And diseases are concentrated in some groups—for example, sickle cell anemia mainly in those of West African descent. This would suggest that drugs should be designed for specific racial groups such as African Americans. The problem is that drugs will be developed for groups with the money to buy them, with fewer resources going into developing drugs for illnesses that disproportionately affect black Americans. Likewise DNA dragnets in the U.S. have a racialized character. He argued in 2006 (*American Sociological Review*) that African Americans in key age groups have a homicide rate twelve times that of whites, which historically has been incorrectly explained by genetic factors of those at the lowest strata of society.[6] Also in 2006 Duster claimed that DNA analysis of crime scene data will assist criminal investigations by narrowing the search for suspects along racial lines.[7] The core of this idea dates back to the eugenics movement in the U.S., and ultimately to the Nazis.

In the late 2000s, Troy continued to investigate the ways in which race as a genetic concept was conflated with race as a social construct. He noted many commercial companies concede that race is not genetically determined but nevertheless argue that race is determined by one's DNA instead of historical, cultural, and economic contexts.[8] In 2008 he noted that some researchers use brain imaging to capture the origins of black violence while ignoring the unscrupulous behavior of business executives, proving that a social concept of race prevails over supposedly objective genetic factors.[9]

Also in 2008 Troy observed that in recent years a number of studies emerged that used biological population differences and thus the genetics of race began to resurface.[10] The problem is that race-based research and marketing risks being misinterpreted as genetic differences in response to drugs among culturally defined racial groups. In 2010 (*Chronicle of Higher Education*) Duster returned to an analysis of protection of human subjects.[11] That year Berkeley announced plans to ask all incoming freshman to voluntarily provide their DNA for genetic testing, a policy that involved certain types of social coercion. In 2011 (Hastings) Duster contended that overpolicing of minority groups led to them being overrepresented in DNA databases as well as in prison populations.[12]

In 2003 Duster also published a book chapter ("The Hidden Eugenic Potential of Germ-Line Interventions") about the lack of training about racial issues among biologists who use medical experimentation that focuses on certain groups.[13] Duster mentioned the infamous Tuskegee study and also one that administered approximately twice the number of X-rays to black study participants compared to white participants. In 2008 he wrote more about DNA databases.[14] Here Duster reports that in 2007 the governor of New York announced plans to expand the requirement of taking DNA samples from sex offenders and murderers to all those convicted of even minor crimes, including minor drug offenses. Because, for example, more blacks are arrested for possession of marijuana—even though whites are more likely to actually be in possession of marijuana—this new policy would affect blacks disproportionately. In 2006 he wrote about behavioral geneticists who are attempting to locate genetic markers that can be associated with crime of all types.[15] The disproportionate arrest and incarceration of black Americans makes this type of project extremely problematic. Finally in 2011 Troy tackled the DNA ancestry industry, which for many African Americans takes on a spiritual meaning when attempting to link themselves to Africans who were brought to these shores as slaves.[16] However, Henry Louis Gates Jr., after some personal disappointments in ancestor tracing, has become a critic of the industry conducting the DNA testing. Duster concludes that "computer generated data provide an appearance of precision that is dangerously seductive and equally misleading."[17]

Troy Duster's NYU-era publications wrestled with the biological issue of DNA testing. He asked the primary question regarding the similarities and differences among blacks and whites. While he notes that there is no doubt that there exist great similarities between the races, it is also true that in the U.S. there are significant consequences based on the social construction of the races.

In 2001 Duster approvingly observed that while John Kitsuse and Aaron Cicourel's paper on the misuse of official statistics, exploring as it did the societal reaction to crime, was rejected for publication by the *ASR, AJS,* and *Social Forces,* it was finally published by the new journal *Social Problems.*[18] This new journal also published Marxist-oriented and ethnomethodological articles. In 2005 Craig Calhoun and Duster noted that unlike the East Coast establishment sociology departments, on the West Coast departments achieved prominence by appearing to be politically and academically far to the left.[19] In 2007 (*Chronicle of Higher Education*) Duster observed a grow-ing use of the hangman's noose as a symbol of racial oppression.[20] Concur-rent with this growth has been the rapid exodus of Southern whites from the Democratic Party and a growing attraction of the Ku Klux Klan. Next, in 2009 (*Thought and Action*) Duster observed that in 1967 only 2 percent of African Americans attending universities were enrolled in traditionally white institutions while by 1975 the majority of black students were attending white universities.[21] Duster observed that similar processes had occurred in India and South Africa. These comparisons show that elites in every nation resist changes in their entitlements.

A few publications during Troy's NYU tenure say nothing about DNA. A book chapter published in 2001 reported that the family net worth for black Americans was a tenth of that of whites.[22] Using South Africa as a point of comparison Duster argued that after fifty years of apartheid allowing whites to secure massive wealth and land it did not seem fair for them to now argue for a color-blind society. In 2003 he coauthored *Whitewashing Race: The Myth of a Color-Blind Society* with six other coauthors.[23] This book contains a litany of racial abuses and it is thus difficult to know what to attribute to Troy Duster except that the book emphasizes that we do not live in a postra-cial or color blind society.

FORMER NYU STUDENTS

At NYU as at Berkeley, Troy had productive relationships with many talent-ed grad students. Alondra Nelson, now in the sociology department at Co-lumbia University, describes her studies with Troy:

> I was a fourth or fifth year graduate student at NYU when Troy arrived in
> 1999. He helped me enormously with my dissertation on the Black Panther

Party's health program, which came out in 2011 as a book. Troy always attempted to make sure that policies didn't increase inequality. While he was at NYU he was a member of the Institute for the Production of Knowledge, and in that capacity he brought in acclaimed scholars from around the world and always insisted that we meet these folks as equals without any sense of hierarchy. This changed my life. He welcomed all comers even though he had strong opinions.[24]

Danielle Bessett, now at the sociology department at the University of Cincinnati, also commented on the influence of Troy Duster:

> I attended NYU from 1998 to 2008. I audited a course on Human Taxonomy from Troy as a graduate student and he directed my dissertation. He was a very sensitive member added to my committee after my first chair died. My first chair was a woman and Troy never tried to go beyond what he knew. I was doing research on birth control and he was always ready to admit his limitations when I sought his advice. He took care of the theoretical scaffolding for the research.[25]

Aaron Panofsky was in the NYU graduate sociology program and later at UCLA. He recalled that he entered the NYU graduate program in 1998, one year prior to Troy joining the faculty. Troy agreed to become his advisor along with Craig Calhoun who served as his coadvisor:

> I took two courses from Troy at NYU, The Sociology of Knowledge and an interdisciplinary course titled Reimagining the Human Social Divide. After I completed my PhD I had a post-doc at Berkeley. Troy had me to dinner at his house and drove me around to show me the local sights. He allowed others to use his car when he was out of town. Troy even lent his house to others for dinner while he could not be there. He is incredibly generous.
>
> Troy did not create a major sociological theory; rather his major contribution was in connecting ideas to one another and in the ethical and political implications of his work. He was not a racist even though many of his students were people of color. After all, I was his student and I am very white. Troy had a reputation among graduate students as being a "fixer." He worked with a student who had burned through many previous advisors in her conflict-oriented dissertation research. Troy ultimately accepted her as an advisee and she graduated. This provides another illustration of Troy Duster's generosity.[26]

Troy's relationship with Aaron Panofsky shows that although he worked with many graduate students of color, this was not a litmus test to work with him.

SYLLABI FOR TEACHING AT BERKELEY AND NYU

In the appendix there are syllabi from an undergraduate course (Deviance and Social Control) and two graduate seminars (Sociology of Knowledge/ Science and the Sociology of Law) that Troy regularly taught while at Berkeley and NYU. Troy was asked to comment on these syllabi but he demurred saying that "there is always a tendency in retrospect to see much more purposeful linear thinking about a syllabus than was present at the time it was crafted . . . let the syllabi play the role of speaking [directly] to the questions."[27]

Doing as Troy Duster requested we see what was involved in the syllabi. It is not surprising that race plays a significant role in all the syllabi. Most students Troy worked with were not studying deviance, law, or knowledge and thus were not involved in these courses; were working with Troy because he provided a friendly face in an otherwise hostile environment. The three syllabi also show the types of concepts used in the courses.

The required books for Deviance and Social Control and for the Sociology of Law include *Order, Law and Crime* by Raymond Michalowski.[28] As a sociologist Michalowski is far to the left. Another book required for the Deviance and Social Control course is *Crack in America: Demon Drugs and Social Justice* by Craig Reinarman and Harry Levine.[29] This book represents a constructionist approach, considering crack use as being involved in a moral panic. James Coleman's *The Criminal Elite: Understanding White Collar Crime*[30] was also listed on the syllabus for the course on Deviance and Social Control. The book mentions occupational crime such as embezzlement but also organizational crime such as tax evasion, political bribery, and production of unsafe products. In all courses it is easy to see the importance of writing, and in the Deviance and Social Control course fieldwork is required, specifically attendance at a jury trial. This requirement carried with it an emphasis on qualitative data and an interactive approach to human behavior.

The Sociology of Law course includes consideration of "imposed" law as well as how law can be shaped by "social, economic, and political conditions." Among the required books listed is one edited by Kemberle Crenshaw, Neil Gotanda, Gary Peller, and Kendall Thomas, *Critical Race Theory* (1995), which was used by Troy to illustrate how law can be imposed.[31] Discussion of three essays, which were picked a random, give some sense of the nature of this encyclopedic tome. A piece by Derrick Bell on the *Brown v. Board of Education* discusses the fact that long after the decision, most black children attend schools that are inferior to those attended by whites. A selection by Charles Lawrence on unconscious racism takes as a point of departure the classroom use of the children's book *Little Black Sambo*. Finally, an entry by Cheryl Harris titled "Whiteness as Property" demonstrates that white identity conferred economic benefits, including legal rights. In another book required for the Sociology of Law the first chapter deals with "Policing Race and Class."[32] A later chapter covers "The Color of Punishment" and racism in the use of the death penalty, in the war on drugs, and in three strikes legislation. The Sociology of Law syllabus also required a book (Kairys 1998) with chapters on "Law and Race in Early America, "Antidiscrimination Law 1954 to 1989," and "Race and Affirmative Action."[33]

The Sociology of Science syllabus features Barbara Katz Rothman's *Genetic Maps and Human Imaginations,* which includes discussions on American racism and *The Bell Curve.*[34] One subsection of the book begins with the question and answer "Is it possible to maintain the concept of race without being racist? I don't think so."[35] Even though none of these courses— Deviance and Social Control, the Sociology of Law, and the Sociology of Science—deal directly with race and racism, all three have a strong racial component in the required readings. For Troy, the issue of race in America touches nearly every fact of life and society.

PERSONAL LIFE IN NEW YORK CITY

While at NYU Troy lived in a Greenwich Village (West Village) co-op apartment building, located at 29 Washington Square West.[36]

Figure 5.1. While at NYU Troy lived in a Greenwich Village (West Village) co-op apartment building, located at 29 Washington Square West.

Figure 5.2. Babbo Italian restaurant, a favorite entertaining spot.

Figure 5.3. West Village French restaurant Le Gigot.

Figure 5.4. 11 Bucco, in Greenwich Village.

As noted above Troy received a Ford Foundation grant to periodically bring New York City scholars together. He often held these meetings, where people such as Barbara Katz Rothman were in attendance, at respected restaurants. One of Troy's favorite restaurants for this entertaining was the Babbo Italian restaurant around the corner from his hotel. Troy was also a frequent diner at the West Village French restaurant Le Gigot and at the Mediterranean restaurant 11 Bucco, in Greenwich Village. In these meetings at great restaurants, Troy's passion for bringing people and ideas together is evident, just as it was to his grad students.

NOTES

1. Troy Duster, telephone interview with John Galliher, March 17, 2013.
2. Troy Duster, email to John Galliher, January 27, 2013.
3. Craig Calhoun, 2013.
4. Troy Duster, "Buried Alive: The Concept of Race in Science," *Chronicle of Higher Education*, September 14, 2001.
5. Troy Duster, "Sociological Stranger in the Land of the Human Genome Project," *Contexts* 1 (August 2002): 69–70; Duster, "The Reality of Race [Preview]," *Scientific American*, January 13, 2003; Pilar Ossorio and Troy Duster, "Race and Genetics: Controversies in Biomedical, Behavioral, and Forensic Sciences," *American Psychologist* 60, no. 1 (2005): 115–128.
6. Troy Duster, "Comparative Perspectives and Competing Explanations: Taking on the Newly Configured Reductionist Challenge to Sociology," *American Sociological Review* 71 (2006): 1–15.
7. Troy Duster, "The Molecular Reinscription of Race: Unanticipated Issues in Biotechnology and Forensic Science," *Patterns of Prejudice* 40 (2006): 427–441.
8. Deborah A. Bolnick, Duana Fullwiley, Troy Duster, et al., "The Science and Business of Genetic Ancestry Testing," *Science*, October 19, 2007, 399–400.

9. Troy Duster, "What Were They Thinking," *Chronicle of Higher Education*, October 10, 2008.

10. Joan H. Fujimura, Troy Duster, and Ramya Rajagopalan, "Questions of Evidence, Matters of Consequence," *Social Studies of Science* 38 (2008): 643–656.

11. Troy Duster, "Welcome Freshman: DNA Swabs, Please," *The Chronicle of Higher Education*, May 28, 2010.

12. Osagie K. Obasogie and Troy Duster, "All That Glitters Isn't Gold," *Hastings Center Report* 41 (September/October 2011).

13. Troy Duster, "The Hidden Eugenic Potential of Germ-Line Interventions," in Designing our Descendants: The Promises and Perils of Genetic Modifications, ed. Audrey R. Chapman and Mark S. Frankel, 156–178 (Baltimore: Johns Hopkins University Press, 2003).

14. Troy Duster, "Social Issues Lurking in the Over-Representation of Young African American Men in the Expanding DNA Databases," in *Against the Wall: Poor, Young, Black and Male*, ed. Elijah Anderson, 181–197 (Philadelphia: University of Pennsylvania Press, 2008).

15. Troy Duster, "Behavioral Genetics and Explanations of the Link between Crime, Violence, and Race," in *Wrestling with Behavioral Genetics: Science, Ethics and Public Conversation*, ed. Erik Parens, Aubrey R. Chapman and Nancy Press, 150–175 (Baltimore: Johns Hopkins University Press, 2006).

16. Troy Duster, "Ancestry Testing and DNA: Uses, Limits, and Caveat Emptor," in *Race and the Genetic Revolution: Science, Myth, and Culture*, ed. Sheldon Krimsky and Kathleen Sloan, 99–116 (New York: Columbia University Press, 2011).

17. Duster, "Ancestry Testing and DNA," 106.

18. Troy Duster, "The Epistemological Challenge of the Early Attack on 'Rate Construction'," *Social Problems* 48 (2001): 134–136.

19. Craig Calhoun and Troy Duster, "The Visions and Divisions of Sociology," *The Chronicle of Higher Education,* August 12, 2005.

20. Troy Duster, "How to Read a Noose," *Chronicle of Higher Education*, November 9, 2007, 1050–1051.

21. Troy Duster, "The Long Path to Higher Education for African Americans," *Thought and Action* (2009): 99–110.

22. Troy Duster, "The 'Morphing' Properties of Whiteness," in *The Making and Unmaking of Whiteness*, ed. Brigit Brander Rasmussen et al., 113–137 (Durham, NC: Duke University Press, 2001).

23. Michael Brown, Martin Carnoy, Elliott Currie, Troy Duster, David B. Oppenheimer, Majorie M. Shultz, and David Wellman, *Whitewashing Race: The Myth of a Color-Blind Society* (Berkeley: University of California Press, 2003).

24. Alondra Nelson, telephone interview with John Galliher, January 26, 2013.

25. Daniele Bessett, telephone interview with John Galliher, February 15, 2013.

26. Aaron Panofsky, telephone interview with John Galliher, February 2, 2013.

27. Troy Duster, email to John Galliher, March 21, 2014.

28. Raymond J. Michalowski, *Order, Law and Crime* (New York: Random House, 1985).

29. Craig Reinarman and Harry G. Levine, *Crack in America: Demon Drugs and Social Justice* (Berkeley: University of California Press, 1997).

30. James C. Coleman, *The Criminal Elite: The Sociology of White Collar Crime*, 2nd ed. (New York: St. Martin's Press, 1989).

31. Kimberle Crenshaw et al., eds., *Critical Race Theory: The Key Writings That Formed the Movement* (New York: The New Press, 1995).

32. David Cole, *No Equal Justice: Race and Class in the American Criminal Justice System* (New York: The New Press, 1999).

33. David Kairys, ed., *The Politics of Law: A Progressive Critique* (New York: Basic Books, 1998).

34. Barbara Kath Rothman, *Genetic Maps and Human Imaginations* (New York: W.W. Norton, 1998).

35. Rothman, *Genetic Maps and Human Imaginations,* 57.

36. Troy Duster, email to John Galliher, January 27, 2013, telephone interview with John Galliher, March 17, 2013.

Chapter Six

Conclusion

It is easy to understand what made Troy Duster such a successful sociologist and professor. Many factors pointed toward it, including the academic success of his siblings and the intellectual fame of his grandmother. However, in a racist society, riddled by inequality, it could easily have been otherwise. Hobbs writes about *The Short and Tragic Life of Robert Peace*.[1] Robert Peace was a poor but gifted young black male who was a native of the ghetto of East Orange, New Jersey. He graduated from the Catholic St. Benedicts Preparatory School in Newark and from Yale University in New Haven, Connecticut. To help pay his college bills Robert was aided by scholarships and worked as a custodian, much as Troy Duster had done making beds at Northwestern. Like Troy Duster beforehand, Robert Peace had mostly white friends during his college years.

Robert Peace was a student who excelled in high school and college, majoring in biochemistry at Yale. He was also a gifted athlete. Shortly after graduating from Yale Robert planned on going to graduate school and becoming a college professor. If anything he was ahead of Troy at this point, comparing Yale to Northwestern and public schools in south Chicago to the private Catholic academies of New Jersey. But unlike Troy, Robert Peace grew up without a father (since his dad was imprisoned for murder) and never attended graduate school. He became immersed in marijuana trafficking and died at the hands of drug traffickers at the age of only thirty. In the final analysis when comparing Troy Duster with Robert Peace it is clear that Robert was brought down by drug trafficking. An activity beyond the law, by definition, offers few guarantees or protections, especially for the poor.

ACADEMIC CAREER: BERKELEY

Troy's academic career ranged from Riverside to Sweden to Berkeley and
New York University as well as untold additional short-term positions and
panels. He was at Berkeley for over thirty years, from 1965 to 1999.
Throughout his career at both Berkeley and NYU Troy taught half of his
courses at the undergraduate level and the other half at the graduate level. At
the undergraduate level he taught Social Control and Deviance (for in excess
of twenty years), Social Movements, and Introduction to Sociology. Graduate courses included Sociology of Science, Sociology of Law, Deviance and
Control, Social Movements, and Field Research Methods. At Berkeley the
size of the black student body was in the 1960s very small but was now
significantly larger after 2000.

As a professor at Berkeley, he was a part of departmental politics. He was
one of the "gang of four" faculty members who routinely voted with the
graduate students on personnel matters. When his colleague Robert Blauner
and Troy decided to teach a theory course on Frantz Fanon, a black Marxist
philosopher, some of their colleagues vehemently disagreed. Troy argued
that when a black graduate student performed poorly you have to be willing
to fail them but if there is any chance of success, "you've got to leave the
door open for this person to come back, to take the exam again."

While at Berkeley, Troy worked closely with University and student leaders, for example during the Third World Strike (involving black and brown
students). He was director of the American Cultures requirement and also
director of the Institute for the Study of Social Change and the campus
Diversity Project head. He always fought for rights at Berkeley for women
and people of color. In the 1990s the Ida B. Wells Memorial Foundation was
established with a generous donation with Troy as the director. Each year a
person is recognized based on creative reporting for social justice for African
Americans. Also, beginning in the early 1970s Troy was the director of the
NIMH training program for graduate students and was key in securing support when the Reagan administration was attempting to cut the funding for
the program. He was appointed chair of the sociology department in 1985.

ACADEMIC CAREER: NYU

Troy left Berkeley for NYU in 1999, where he was eventually named Silver
Professor of Sociology. While he was at NYU he was a member of the
Institute for the Production of Knowledge and later led the organization. In
that capacity he brought in acclaimed scholars from around the world and
always insisted that graduate students meet these folks as equals without any
sense of hierarchy. He welcomed all comers even though he had strong

opinions. At NYU Troy also secured Ford funding to convene the New York Consortium on Science and Society. Many joined in the lively dinner gatherings he hosted that concentrated on issues of behavior, race, gender, and science.

PUBLIC POSITIONS AND SERVICE

Outside of teaching and directing university-based programs, Troy served on many panels and boards, both at Berkeley and NYU and in the years since his retirement. Troy was appointed to The President's Commission on Mental Health, The Committee on Habitual Behavior and Substance Abuse at the National Academy of Sciences, and the Science Advisory Panel for Research on Violence at the National Institutes of Health. From 1993 to 1997 he was a working group member for the Ethical, Legal and Social Issues arm of the Human Genome Project (chair 1996–1997); from 1995 to 1999 he served on the National Advisory Council for the Human Genome Project; and in 2014 he was appointed to serve on the first National Commission on Forensic Science. In the fall of 2014 he was headed back to the London School of Economics as a visiting professor after having held a Guggenheim there early in his career.

These public appointments and service were very important to Troy. Troy recalled that when he was a graduate student "I once had a very good professor who gave me some very bad advice. 'Don't read newspapers. Don't listen to the news. It's simply a daily phenomenon that will get in the way of scholarship' that consisted of the theorist writing that was disengaged from the world." Instead Duster became an engaged or "plugged-in" scholar dealing with racial implications of drug laws and genetic research.[2]

RESEARCH INTERESTS

While he was a student at UCLA Troy became enchanted with Harold Garfinkel and his sociology of freedom vs. the sociology of control. Being drawn to this sociologist demonstrates that Troy was attracted to a specific type of sociology that continues to influence him over half a century later. The influence of UCLA statistician Bill Robinson has also been profound. Troy had taken Robinson's seriously warnings about the misplaced precision of statistics. Aaron Panofsky, who was a student of Troy's from both NYU and Berkeley, noted that Duster's research contributions were in connecting ideas to one another and in the ethical and political implications of his work.

Troy's career reflects the changes in his own interests over the course of the decades of teaching and publishing. His early focus was on mental health and deviance. Troy recalled his Guggenheim at the London School of Economics in 1971–72:

> I had just published *The Legislation of Morality,* and was invited to give a series of lectures on the emerging drug war. I especially remember the York Conference on Deviance in which a number of British and European scholars presented new challenges to old assumptions about how social scientists can and should approach the subject of deviant behavior. The emerging consensus among a very large group was that social scientists should turn their lenses upon people who get to occupy the category of 'normal'—and pursue how and when they classify others as 'deviants.'"[3]

At Berkeley his focus shifted toward racial issues. He wrote on topics as diverse as protecting human subjects in research studies, discrimination in housing, and the impact of race in the criminal justice system. In 1987 he wrote, "at the same time that Black youth are typically seen as the most likely perpetrators of crime, Black youth are, . . . also the group hardest hit by unemployment."[4] Despite the attempts of conservative to dismiss the relationship between unemployment and crime, Duster argued that this relationship in point of fact did exist.

During these years Troy wrote quite a bit about affirmative action. Efforts to bring in black perspectives were often challenged. In the fall of 1968 there was a course to be taught by Eldridge Cleaver. Governor Reagan had demanded that it should carry no credit. There were conflicts over the degree of autonomy that the black studies department should have. In the late 1960s Chancellor Roger Heynes said that he could not permit an all-black, black studies program, despite the existence at the time of an all-white political science department.[5]

Troy argued in *The American Sociologist* in 1976 that opponents of affirmative action have ignored the history that preceded the program, including the exclusion of blacks from both membership in corporations and unions.[6] Twenty years later, he addressed the priority given to blacks over whites in admission to UC Berkeley; according to Duster fairness can only be addressed if one considers that white families have for many decades been free to accumulate wealth many times greater than true of black families.[7] Duster's unique perspective also asks the reader to reason in a forward fashion.

In later years Troy became particularly concerned with the genetic conception of race in opposition to a socially constructed conception of race. On November 6, 2014, Troy also gave the annual lecture for the *British Journal of Sociology* in London. In that presentation, later published in their journal, Troy once again addressed the conflation of genetic-based race and socially constructed race.[8] He noted that the Human Genome Project showed that all humans were 99.9 percent genetically identical but that race as a social fact affects many of the outcomes that might mistakenly be attributed to genetics:

"The different rates of prostate cancer between blacks and whites can be studied scientifically by geneticists trying to understand population differences . . . but we can also study the systematic pattern of African Americans living close to toxic waste dumps across the whole country."[9] These environmental differences have nothing to do with biology and everything to do with environment.

CURRENT EVENTS

At a recent meeting celebrating Troy's career, many presenters mentioned the killing and riots in the community of Ferguson, Missouri. A recent online posting by a black man who is an engineer and a native of Ferguson (currently living in Reno, Nevada) likely explains what they had in mind:

> I'm from Ferguson, Missouri. Rode on my bike to the grocery store and library. First job at . . . Mama D's Soul Food Café. Central School and Ferguson Middle School. It was a little boring, but quite beautiful.
> And yet . . . I was nearly kicked off a plane recently, with my family (and white wife), because a flight attendant "felt threatened." There was the condescension of the police officer who spat "brother" to me while looking for someone else. I see a police car or officer and wonder when it will be my turn.
> My inclination would be to inveigh against the looters and the rioters. I decline. Though their actions are base, their anger is righteous and I am just as angry. I am tired of the background of fear of being caught in the dragnet that is racism and prejudice.
> It is easy and obvious to focus on the mad behavior of the looting and rioting. But try living in fear of the consequences of endemic racism and prejudice that is visited on minorities in this country. Try living in fear that someone in your family may be shot . . . because someone felt threatened.[10]

This statement represents the concerns that Troy wrestled with his entire career. Troy Duster discussed the June 2014 issue of *The Atlantic* whose cover story by Ta-Nehisi Coates made the case for reparations to be paid to African Americans.[11] In the article Coates discusses various immoralities forced upon African Americans including slavery, lynching, and segregated schools (in spite of the *Brown v. Board of Education of Topeka* Supreme Court decision); but he concentrates on housing practices in Chicago, including the refusal to sell African Americans housing in white neighborhoods, a practice sometimes referred to as "redlining." This system went hand in glove with the practice of "contract for deed," which involved contracts selling a property for many times its value. As a consequence these sellers became very wealthy and a large Chicago ghetto was created. Up until the present time these blatantly racist practices of realtors and banks have been upheld by the American courts. In a later book (2015) Coates mentions the murders of Trayvon Martin, Michael Brown, and Eric Garner, killings that went unpunished, the slave ships that brought many black Americans to this land, Malcolm X's prophesies, and the black cultural icon James Baldwin. [12]

Troy Duster has been involved in the issues of day throughout his lifetime. As a youth Troy had lived the redlining and other racist practices, and thus it is no surprise that in 2005 he called for a public apology from the U.S. government to African Americans. [13] In the early 1960s Medgar Evers was also murdered (1963),and the same year that Troy moved to Berkeley (1965) there was the LA Watts race riot. In 1968 the US Kerner Commission Report on the causes of urban riots was released. There was also the police beating in LA of Rodney King that occurred in 1992. There were the 1968 killings of Malcolm X and Dr. Martin Luther King. These and other indignities and additional assassinations of American civil rights leaders undoubtedly had a profound impact on Troy Duster.

In addition, as a sociologist of law Troy was quite familiar with the racist character of the American war on drugs. This system includes the racial distinction between the punishment for crack and powder cocaine offenses. Punishments for sale and possession are many times greater for crack the typical drug of choice for blacks than for powder cocaine, the typical drug chosen by whites. It is also well known that whites with a record of conviction of a drug offense are less likely than blacks with no record to experience obstacles in job seeking. Knowledge of all of these helps explain why Troy was always ready to assist and protect minority graduate students.

FRIENDS AND ACQUAINTANCES

When Duster was elected president of the American Sociological Association (ASA), two long-time friends, Harry Levine and Craig Reinarman, wrote a profile of him in *ASA Footnotes.* [14] This essay discussed everything from his gourmet kitchen in the Berkeley house where he entertained his friends over the years to the many minority graduate students that he mentored. His friends included Thelton Henderson, a recently retired federal judge who was a frequent guest at his house, along with the famous gang of four at Berkeley (David Matza, Arlie Hochschild, Robert Blauner, David Wellman), who all supported graduate student interests. Another friend and colleague was Craig Calhoun at NYU who published an article with Troy in the *Chronicle of Higher Education* in 2005 on how elite rankings of East Coast and West Coast departments differ. [15] It is a tribute to Troy's winning personality that very few people have been considered antagonists in his career; one exception was Seymour Martin Lipset, the conservative professor who clashed with Troy on numerous issues.

CELEBRATING TROY DUSTER: CONFERENCE

On August 15, 2014, on the Berkeley campus there was a daylong celebration of the life and career of Troy Duster.[16] The group in attendance consisted of around a hundred in the audience with twenty-one presenters. Those presenting came from many walks of life, including sociologists, anthropologists, law professors, a judge, a restaurateur; but primarily they were former advisees of Troy's at Berkeley and NYU. Sandra Smith was a black woman and not a former student of Troy's, but rather a colleague at NYU and later at Berkeley; she recalled that in 2001 they saw the Twin Towers collapse from Washington Park (near the NYU campus) and held each other tightly during this horrific tragedy. David Wellman recalled that at Berkeley Bob Blauner was refused promotion to professor by senior professors because he had published *Racial Oppression in America,* condemning domestic racism. The senior professors then went to Troy, suggesting promotion to him, but Troy refused their offer until Blauner was promoted. The next year Blauner was promoted as was Troy. Troy's refusal of the initial offer of promotion says a lot about the man, his commitment to ideas, and loyalty to his friends.

Duana Fullwiley of Stanford University's anthropology department, who helped organize the session, presented a paper on Troy and recalled, "I met Troy when I knocked on his door in 1993 to ask him to work with me. I was writing my undergraduate thesis on the California 'Three Strikes' law that was being prepared for the ballot and that passed in 1994."[17] She noted that Troy is also a Senior Fellow at the Warren Institute on Law and Social Policy at the Boalt Law School—UC Berkeley, chaired the department from 1985 to 1988, and while chair oversaw a significant increase in the number of female faculty. In 1979 he founded the Institute for the Study of Social Change (now called the Institute for the Study of Societal Issues—ISSC), which he directed for eighteen years until 1997. At the ISSC he led a project demonstrating how the composition of Berkeley students had changed so dramatically from the 1960s to the 1990s under affirmative action. From this work he and others published "The Diversity Project," which received national attention in *The New York Times.* Troy wrote several articles on the general topic of the transformation of higher education and, as a direct result, was appointed to the board of directors of the Association of American Colleges and Universities (ACCU). He served on the board from 1997–2003. Troy was elected chair of the AACU board in 2002. He subsequently joined the Tri-National Commission studying how South Africa, India, and Brazil were coping with the massive transformations of their own universities.

Several of the presenters at this conference compared Troy's work with the work of Nicholas Wade (2014).[18] As a constructionist sociologist Troy claimed that races are over 99% identical and that racial groups represent social categories created by human beings. Wade, on the other hand, a journalist who holds a BA degree, believed that races are created by evolution and genes. According to Wade science has located "three major races": African, Asian, and white (Wade 2014, 104). In addition "human skulls fall into three distinctive shapes, which reflect their owners' degree of ancestry in the three main races."[19] According to Wade most Europeans carry skin-lightening characteristics and almost all Africans have a biologically determined quality that darkens their skin. Small wonder that Tory and his friends would disagree with these assertions by Wade. If anything, Troy's vision of race would be encouraged by racial passing—either blacks passing as white or in the less common instance of whites passing as black. According to Troy and most sociologists, racial boundaries are quite permeable.

FINAL THOUGHTS

Troy Duster was hired at just the right time by UC Berkeley in 1965. Earlier he may have gone to a predominantly black institution. In the final analysis it is clear that Berkeley attempted to hire only some available faculty. It goes without saying that as a top-ranked public institution only well-published faculty were sought out. But the university also wanted progressives or liberals such as Robert Blauner who had a communist background. And Troy Duster was also perfect for Berkeley. Troy Duster has a long history of African American intellectuals behind him, including his maternal grandmother Ida B. Wells, a Southern journalist who spoke out frequently against lynching. While Troy is also part of a lineage of American sociologists, only Alfred Lindesmith, who was an early twentieth-century sociologist, interested in the sociology of drug laws as was originally true of the research of Troy.

Unless one has experienced being born poor and black one can only imagine what it must be like. At a minimum black Americans can wonder if cabs that refuse to stop for them do so because the cabs are busy with a fair or because they are black potential passengers. And in restaurants poor service by a waiter may be because of indifference or overwork or racism. Troy was born into poverty and into a racial caste system in South Chicago. He also experienced racism at Northwestern University and the racial exclusion of the university's fraternity system and the racism of the Evanston police. Troy also experienced racism since he was rejected for a Chicago janitor's job due to his race, after being nominated for the position by his Irish friend Jack Doyle. Troy later had additional experiences with racist motel operators and law enforcement in Joplin, Missouri, and owners of rental property in Los Angeles, California. He also experienced the rancid racism of Riverside, California. And as an expert in the sociology of law Troy knew well the racism of the police and the courts. But in spite of being poor and black in

Chicago, all of his siblings graduated from college. Perhaps his mother or the model of his grandmother, Ida B. Wells, made a difference.

Ray Mack at Northwestern and Arthur Stinchcombe at UC Berkeley helped him along the way in becoming a distinguished scholar. Perhaps more significantly Troy has during his adult life not become hard or mean spirited, but has been generous with people of color as well as whites, and both men and women, if his patterns of graduate student mentoring are any reflection of this openness. It may be that people of color are overrepresented among his students, but progressive whites were also drawn to him.

Some claim that we live in a postracial society where class is more important than race. Even assuming that is not true it is a fact that racism is often more subtle than it once was. And to tell the entire truth it may be that there are a few (but very few) benefits from being poor and black in the academic community. Early on, while Troy was still an undergraduate at Northwestern Troy got help from the Pullman Scholarship. It was a significant need-based financial assistance to minority students. Teaching positions may have been opened to Troy based on his ethnicity as well as a few grant and publication opportunities. These small benefits pale, however, in comparison with the continual racist assaults that he and other blacks experienced.

Despite the challenges of being a black man in America, Troy Duster thrived and became an important scholar, a beloved mentor to many students, and a warm and treasured friend. His legacy is apparent not only in his writing and the programs he helped established, but in the many lives that he influenced and the many fine scholars who were inspired by Troy's teaching and mentorship.

NOTES

1. Jeff Hobbs, *The Short and Tragic Life of Robert Peace: A Brilliant Young Man Who Left Newark for the Ivy League* (New York: Scribner, 2014).

2. Barry Bergman, "Troy Duster's Garden of Plugged-in Scholarship, and How It Grew," *Berkeley News*, August 20, 2014, http://news.berkeley.edu/2014/08/20/troy-duster-celebration/

3. Troy Duster, email to John Galliher, August 22, 2014.

4. Troy Duster, "Youth Unemployment and the Black Urban Underclass," *Crime and Delinquency* 33 (1987): 300–316, 301.

5. Troy Duster, "An Oral History with Troy Duster," interview conducted by Richard Cándida Smith and Nadine Wilmot, 2002–2003, Regional Oral History Office, The Bancroft Library, University of California, Berkeley, 2012, 104.

6. Troy Duster, 1976.

7. Troy Duster, 1996.

8. Troy Duster, "A Post-genomic Surprise: The Molecular Reinscription of Race in Science, Law and Medicine," *British Journal of Sociology* 66 (2015): 1–27.

9. Duster, "A Post-genomic Surprise," 6.

10. Edward Allen, "Growing Up in Ferguson, Missouri," email, October 14, 2014.

11. Ta-Nehisi Coates, "The Case for Reparations," *The Atlantic,* June 2014, 54–71.

12. Ta-Nehisi Coates, *Between the World and Me* (New York: Spiegel and Grau, 2015).

13. Amy Goodman and Juan González. "Senate Apologizes for Not Enacting Anti-Lynching Legislation: A Look at Journalist and Anti-Lynching Crusader Ida B. Wells," Democracy Now! A Daily Independent News Hour, June 14, 2005, http://www.democracynow.org/2005/6/14/senate_apologizes_for_not_enacting_anti.

14. Harry Levine and Craig Reinarman, "Profile of the ASA President, Troy Duster: A Biography in History," *ASA Footnotes*, September/October 2004.

15. Troy Duster and Craig Calhoun. "The Visions and Divisions of Sociology," *The Chronicle of Higher Education* 51 (2005).

16. Celebrating Troy Duster, conference, Berkeley, California, August 15, 2014.

17. Duana Fullwiley, email to John Galliher, August 15, 2014.

18. Nicholas Wade, *A Troublesome Inheritance: Genes, Race and Human History* (New York: The Penguin Press, 2014).

19. Wade, *A Troublesome Inheritance,* 70.

Appendix A

Syllabi

DEVIANCE AND SOCIAL CONTROL

Fall 2003
T. Duster

REQUIRED READING

James W. Coleman, *The Criminal Elite: Understanding White Collar Crime,* 4th edition, New York: St. Martin's Press, 1998.

Delos H. Kelly, *Deviant Behavior, A Text-Reader in the Sociology of Deviance*, 5th edition, New York: St. Martin's Press, 1996.

Raymond J. Michalowski, *Order, Law, and Crime,* New York: Random House, 1985.

Craig Reinarman and Harry G. Levine, *Crack in America: Demon Drugs and Social Justice,* Berkeley: University of California Press, 1997.

Recommended Reading

F. Dostoevsky, *Crime and Punishment.*

EVALUATION

Mid-Term Examination: Closed book, with study questions provided for guidance (30 percent of grade).

Term Paper: 30 percent of grade.

Final Examination: Closed book, with study questions provided for guidance (40 percent of grade)

Required Field Notes: With both "thick description" and use of some key
concepts from course, from fieldwork with a criminal jury trial

READING ASSIGNMENTS

Section I. The theoretical properties of deviance

This introductory section of the course will deal with the various ways of
conceiving deviance and normality, among them the *statistical, organic, illness, common sense,* and *moral* conceptions. The various problems to be
addressed include the sociological problem of "normalizing" deviance as a
routine phenomenon of social life.

September 11–13:

Kelly, 1–9, 49–96
Michalowski, Chapter 3

September 18–20:

Kelly, 409–426, 633–645
Coleman, Introduction, 1–13

Section II. The social and political context of deviance

PART ONE: The imputation of deviance is successfully done by some populations and not by others. Mental illness, variable drug use, and different
kinds of crimes will be used to illustrate the substantive problems, while
Ranulf's discussion of *disinterested pursuit of punishment* provides both historical and sociological frameworks. In this segment, we will also address the
subject of the increasing "medicalization of deviance" and its implications
for social control.

September 25–27: Guest Lecture, H. Levine

Kelly, 21–46, 117–172
Reinarman and Levine, 1–15

October 2–4:

Reinarman and Levine, 113–130
Coleman, Chapter 4

October 9–11:

Reinarman and Levine, 260–287
Michalowski, Chapter 1

October 16–18:

Michalowski, Chapters 2, 5

October 23–25:

Reinarman and Levine, 57–76
Michalowski, Chapters 6, 7

Mid-Term Examination: Wednesday, October 25
October 30–November 1:

Kelly, 523–537
Reinarman and Levine, 260–320
Michalowski, Chapter 8

November 6–8:

Kelly, 29–39, 345–361, 451–469
Coleman, Chapter 1

PART TWO (SECTION II): There are macro-structural sources of conflict between groups and large social aggregates that can be converted into either "deviance" or into "political conflict." The politicization of deviance and the criminalization of politics are two topics of increasing empirical investigation in this field.

November 13–15:

Kelly, 339–352, 487–507

November 20–22:

Field research only / no class meetings

November 20–22:

No class; set aside time for your Field Research Requirement; you must spend TWO DAYS in a State Court felony trial (in New York, this would be the Supreme Court).

November 27–29:

Coleman, Chapters 2, 3
Michalowski, Chapters 10, 11

December 4–6:

Kelly, 538–554
Coleman, Chapters 5–7

Reinarman and Levine, 334–366

December 11–13:

Overview and review; audiovisuals in-class only (no new assignments)

REQUIRED FIELD WORK

During the twelfth week of the course, you will be required to spend *two days* observing criminal proceedings. (This assignment can be fulfilled at any point during the semester, but the twelfth week is set aside for the convenience of those who otherwise would have difficulties on other days.) In particular, you will have to observe several hours of a felony prosecution. Any courthouse dealing with state level prosecution will do, but remember, it must be a felony case. Also, it must be a jury trial; it may be in progress, and you need not necessarily observe and report the outcome. It is the social process that should be the focus of your attention. Classes that week will be suspended to provide time.

Students must turn in their field notes by the end of the day, December 1. The notes should contain brief description of the nature of the trial; jury composition (social and demographic characteristics); same for prosecuting and defense attorneys, judge, bailiffs, witnesses, other court officials, observers, and *especially* the halls and corridors. I recommend that you go in pairs, that the two of you record independently your observations, then write a brief note explaining any differences or similarities.

This is a required assignment, meaning that you cannot pass the course without submitting field notes. However, *no* letter grade will be given to the notes. From past experience, most notes will be "adequate" and will simply fulfill the requirement (S/U, satisfactory or unsatisfactory). Every now and again, there are "inadequate notes" and in such instances the student is asked to review the materials with the instructor or assistant and to re-do the assignment. In some instances, an unusually good set of notes can positively influence a "borderline" grade. However, it is important to note again that *this is a requirement, not an extra assignment to improve your grade*.

TERM PAPER

You may choose *any* of the following five topics for a term paper, but you must choose one from among this list. No substitutions. The length should be approximately 15–20 pages, double-spaced.

1. Describe the major arguments, both pro and con, on the use of capital punishment as a deterrent to crime. What kinds of evidence are used

by both sides? In the last decade, what are the most convincing sets of evidence. Defend your position, either pro or con, using a *sociological* argument.

2. The fastest growing sector of the workforce is the skyrocketing employment of private security guards. Describe the current situation with gross statistical narratives. Then contrast private and public (police) employment along those characteristics and attributes (part-time vs. full-time, level of benefits, professional training, etc.) of interest to those who have engaged in social, economic, and political analysis of this trend towards privatization of security. To what special social concerns should we be alerted?

3. There is a movement towards privatization of prisons. Describe the major arguments, both pro and con. What kinds of evidence are used by both sides? In the last decade, what are the most convincing sets of evidence. Defend your position, either pro or con, using a *sociological* argument.

4. Contrast theories of organized crime with the theories of corporate crime you have read. What is the nature of the available evidence to suggest that these are two very fundamentally different, or parallel kinds of enterprises? Make sure that you address institutional and organizational issues, and not just personal ambition or personality structure.

5. Write a paper in which you contrast recent patterns of homicide versus suicide for different socially defined groups (or aggregates); what are the patterns in the data by, for example, age, sex and marital status? Do these patterns fit the theory of Henry and Short? If and when they do not fit the theory, what is a plausible alternative set of sociological explanations?

SOCIOLOGY OF KNOWLEDGE AND SCIENCE

Fall 2000
T. Duster

This course will examine some of the key social, economic, and political underpinnings for the construction and production of knowledge, primarily in science. We will focus upon developments in the literature of the social studies of science, emphasizing the post-Kuhnian accounts of knowledge production. Readings and presentations will include and address a full range of macro-structural and external accounts of influences on science, and move along a continuum to micro-interactional internal ethnographic studies (including close laboratory observational work) that document and assess the daily routines, constraints, and practices of scientists at work.

There will be an extensive bibliography for the course. The list of books below should be available at local booksellers and the library. During the course of the semester, I will distribute or make available other readings—some as indicated in the weekly assignments below.

PARTICIPATION, EVALUATION, PAPERS

This is a *participatory seminar*, and its success depends upon preparation prior to each class session. Each week, depending upon class size, one or two participants will prepare a brief summary paper to lead off a discussion of the week's readings—and two commentators will respond. While these discussants will have primary responsibility, all seminar members are expected to engage in the exchange.

REQUIRED READINGS

Thomas Gieryn, *Cultural Boundaries of Science,* Chicago: U. of Chicago Press, 1999.

Sandra Harding, *Is Science Multi-Cultural?* Bloomington: U. of Indiana Press, 1998.

Karl Mannheim, *Ideology and Utopia: An Introduction to the Sociology of Knowledge,* New York: Harcourt Brace, 1985.

Laura Nader, ed., *Naked Science: Anthropological Inquiry into Boundaries, Power, and Knowledge,* 1996.

Mary Poovey, *A History of the Modern Fact: Problems of Knowledge in the Sciences of Wealth and Society,* Chicago: U. of Chicago Press, 1998.

Barbara Katz Rothman, *Genetic Maps and Human Imaginations: The Limits of Science in Understanding Who We Are,* New York: Norton, 1998.

Stephen E. Toulmin, *Cosmopolis: The Hidden Agenda of Modernity,* New York: Free Press, 1990.

Recommended/Supplemental

Gary Gutting, ed., *Paradigms and Revolutions,* South Bend, IN: U. of Notre Dame Press, 1980.

Sandra Harding, *The Science Question in Feminism,* Ithaca, NY: Cornell University Press, 1986.

Karin Knorr-Cetina and Michael Mulkay, eds., *Science Observed,* Beverly Hills, CA: Sage, 1983.

Andrew Pickering, ed., *Science as Practice and Culture,* Chicago: U. of Chicago Press, 1992.

READING ASSIGNMENTS

Frame, Context, and History

September 19:

Stephen E. Toulmin, *Cosmopolis*, Chapters 1–4

September 26:

Laura Nader, "Anthropological Inquiry into Boundaries, Power, and Knowledge" in *Naked Science,* pp. 1–25

Colin Scott, "Science for the West, Myth for the Rest?" in Nader, *Naked Science,* pp. 69–86

S. Harding, Chapter 1, pp. 1–38

Epistemological Issues

October 3:

Mannheim, Chapter I, II, and V

Sharon Traweek, "Kokusaika, Gaiatsu, and Bachigai: Japanese Physicists' Strategies for Moving into the International Economy of Science, in Nader, *Naked Science,* pp. 174–200

October 10:

Poovey, Chapter 2, pp. 29–92

Transition and Interface of Micro/Macro Concerns

October 17:

J. Fujimura, "Authorizing Knowledge in Science and Anthropology," *American Anthropologist* 100, no. 2 (June 1998): 347–360

Steve Fuller, reply to Fujimura, "Authorizing Science Studies, or Why We Have Never Had Paradigms," *American Anthropologist* 101, no. 2 (June 1999): 1–3

Joan H. Fujimura, reply to Fuller, "Authorizing Science Studies and Anthropology," *American Anthropologist* 101, no. 2 (June 1999): 3–6

Jean Lave, "The Savagery of the Domestic Mind," in Nader, *Naked Science,* pp. 87–100

Micro/Internal

Ethnography, Lab Observation: Advantages and Limits

October 24:

> Knorr-Cetina, "The Couch, The Cathedral, and the Laboratory: On the Relationship between Experiment and Laboratory in Science," in Pickering, *Science as Practice and Culture*, pp. 113–138
> Ian Hacking, "The Self-Vindication of the Laboratory Sciences," in Pickering, *Science as Practice and Culture*, Chapter 2, pp. 29–64

October 31:

> Abstracts of proposed papers due—no class

Macro/External

November 7:

> Poovey, Chapter 5

Science and Feminism

November 14: Science and Social Structure/Culture
November 21: Draft Paper Exchanges/Critiques, no class
November 28: Harding, selected chapters

> Victor A. McKusick, "Mapping and Sequencing the Human Genome," *The New England Journal of Medicine* 120, no. 14 (April 6, 1989)
> Gutting, pp. 297–317

December 5:

> Katz Rothman, *Genetic Maps and Human Imaginations*

December 12: Overview
Papers Due: December 13

SOCIOLOGY OF LAW

Fall 2001
T. Duster

The seminar will address variable social and historical circumstances in which law is "imposed" (Burman and Harrell-Bond, *The Imposition of Law*), and "emerges" (Kairys, *The Politics of Law*, 3rd edition) and, alternatively, the ways in which law shapes and is shaped by social, economic, and political conditions (Nelson, *Marbury v Madison* and Crinshaw et al., *Critical Race Theory*; Hay et al., *Albion's Fatal Tree*).

REQUIRED READING

David Cole, *No Equal Justice,* New York: New Press, 1999.
Kimberle Crinshaw et al., *Critical Race Theory,* New York: The New Press, 1995.
Douglas Hay et al., *Albion's Fatal Tree,* New York: Pantheon.
David Kairys, ed., *The Politics of Law*, 3rd edition, New York: Pantheon, 1998.
William Nelson, *Marbury v Madison: The Origins and Legacy of Judicial Review,* Lawrence: U. of Kansas Press, 2000.

Supplementary Materials

Anthony Amsterdam and Jerome Bruner, *Minding the Law*, Cambridge, MA: Harvard U. Press, 2001.
Pierre Bourdieu, "The Force of Law: Toward a Sociology of the Juridical Field," *The Hastings Law Journal* 38 (July 1987): 814–853.
Sandra B. Burman and Barbara E. Harrell-Bond, *The Imposition of Law,* New York: Academic Press, Chapters 5 and 6.
Clifford Geertz, *Local Knowledge: Further Essays in Interpretive Anthropology,* New York: Basic Books, 1983, Chapter 8.
Angela Harris, "Race and Essentialism in Feminist Legal Theory," *Stanford Law Review* 42 (February 1990): 581–615.
Morton Horowitz, *The Transformation of American Law, 1780–1860*, Cambridge, MA: Harvard U. Press.
Pamela S. Karlan, "Voting Rights and the Court: End of the Second Reconstruction?" *The Nation*, May 23, 1994, 698–700.
J. Wagona Makoba, "On the Use and Application of Legal Concepts in the Study of Non-Western Societies," *International Journal of the Sociology of Law* 20 (1992): 201–223.
Mari J. Matsuda, "Voices of America: Accent, Antidiscrimination Law, and a Jurisprudence for the Last Reconstruction," *The Yale Law Journal* 100, no. 5 (March 1991): 1329–1407.
Raymond J. Michalowski, *Order, Law, and Crime*, New York: Random House.
Laura Nader, "The Anthropological Study of Law," *American Anthropologist* 67, no. 6, part 2 (December 1965): 3–32.
———, "The ADR Explosion: The Implications of Rhetoric in Legal Reform," *Windsor Yearbook of Access to Justice* 8 (1988).

Loic Wacquant, "Deadly Symbiosis: When Ghetto and Prison Meet and Mesh," *Punishment and Society* 3, no. 1 (Winter): 95–134; also available at http://sociology.berkeley.edu/faculty/wacquant/deadlysymbiosis.pdf.

Deborah Woo, "The People v. Fumiko Kimura: But Which People?" *International Journal of the Sociology of Law* 17 (1989): 403–428.

READING ASSIGNMENTS

September 11, *Introduction and Overview*

Section I: Social history and variable conceptions of law in relationship to the social and moral order

Part 1: "Imposition" vs. "Embeddedness"

September 18:

Burman and Harrell-Bond, *The Imposition of Law,* Chapters 5 and 6
Michalowski, *Order, Law, and Crime*, Chapter 3
Horowitz, *The Transformation of American Law, 1780–1860*, Chapters 1 and 2

September 25:

Kairys, ed., *The Politics of Law*, Chapter 1 (Mensch) and Chapter 21 (Horowitz), "The Rise and Early Progressive Critique of Objective Causation," pp. 471–496
Marbury v Madison, Chapters 1,

October 2:

Marbury v Madison, Chapters 3, 4
Michalowski, *Order, Law, and Crime*, Chapters 5, 6

Part 2

October 9: Substantive and Comparative

Hay et al., *Albion's Fatal Tree*, Chapters 1, 2, 5
Laura Nader, "The Recurrent Dialectic Between Legality and its Alternatives"
Geertz, *Local Knowledge,* Chapter 8

October 16: Outline of Papers Due

Laura Nader, "The Anthropological Study of Law" (also see her "Law and Society: Anthropological Aspects")

Freeman, in Crinshaw, ed., *Critical Race Theory*, pp. 29–46

J. Wagona Makoba, "On the Use and Application of Legal Concepts in the Study of Non-Western Societies"

October 23:

Michalowski, *Order, Law, and Crime*, Chapters 1, 2

Hay et al., *Albion's Fatal Tree*, Chapter 6

October 30:

Ranulf

Loic Wacquant, "Deadly Symbiosis"

November 6: *The Living Law* (I)

Michalowski, *Order, Law, and Crime*, Chapters 7, 8

Kairys, ed., *The Politics of Law*, Chapter 2

November 13: *"The Living Law"* (II)

Kairys, ed., *The Politics of Law*, Chapters 5, 14

Neil Gotanda, "A Critique of 'Our Constitution is Colorblind,'" in Crinshaw, ed., *Critical Race Theory*, pp. 257–275

November 20:

No class; library or site research for papers

Angela Harris, "Race and Essentialism in Feminist Legal Theory"

Cheryl Harris, "Whiteness as Property" in Crinshaw, ed., *Critical Race Theory*, pp. 276–291

David Cole, *No Equal Justice*, selected chapters

November 27:

Deborah Woo, "The People v. Fumiko Kimura"

David Cole, *No Equal Justice*, selected chapters

December 4:

Mari J. Matsuda, "Voices of America"

Laura Nader, "The ADR Explosion"

PAPERS DUE: DECEMBER 11

Appendix B

Vita (2012)

TROY DUSTER

Chancellor's Professor and Senior Fellow
Warren Institute on Law and Social Policy
University of California, Berkeley

EDUCATION

Ph.D. Northwestern University, Evanston, Illinois, Sociology, 1962
M.A. University of California, Los Angeles, Sociology, 1959
B.S. Northwestern University, Evanston, Illinois, Journalism, 1957

EMPLOYMENT

Silver Professor, Department of Sociology, New York University, 1999–2012
Professor, Department of Sociology, University of California, Berkeley (1979–99)
Director, Institute for the Study of Social Change, University of California, Berkeley (1979–1997)
Chair, Department of Sociology, University of California, Berkeley (1985–88)

Associate Professor, Department of Sociology, University of California, Berkeley (1970–78)

Assistant Research Sociologist, Center for Research and Development in Higher Education, University of California, Berkeley (1967–70)

Visiting Associate Professor, Department of Sociology, University of British Columbia, Vancouver, B.C., Canada (1969)

Research Sociologist, Pedagogisk-psykologiska institutionen, Stockholm University, Stockholm, Sweden (1966–67)

Assistant Professor, Department of Sociology, University of California, Riverside (1963–65)

PUBLICATIONS

Books and Monographs:

Backdoor to Eugenics, 2nd ed., Routledge, 2003

Whitewashing Race: The Myth of a Colorblind Society," with M. Brown et al., University of California Press, 2003

Race: Essays on the Concept and its Uses in Multi-Racial and Multi-Cultural Societies, FernUniversität, Gesamthochschule in Hagen, 1995

Retour à l'eugénisme, Préface de Pierre Bourdieu, Paris, Editions Kimé, 1992 (French edition of *Backdoor to Eugenics*)

Cultural Perspectives on Biological Knowledge, coedited with Karen Garrett, Alex Publishing Co., 1984

Droga: La Legislazione della Moralita, Guiffre Editore, 1984 (Italian edition of *The Legislation of Morality*)

Economic Development in Berkeley, coedited with David Minkus, Institute for the Study of Social Change, 1983

Impacts of BART on Bay Area Political Institutions, Research Report DOT-BIP-TM 32-6-77 for the U.S. Departments of Transportation and Housing and Urban Development, published by National Technical Information Service, May 1977

Some Conditions of Sustained Participation in Governance, with T. F. Lunsford, Center for Research and Development in Higher Education, 1974

The Legislation of Morality, The Free Press, 1970

Aims and Control of the Universities, Center for Research and Development in Higher Education, 1972

Patterns of Minority Relations, with Raymond W. Mack, Anti-Defamation League, 1964

Articles:

"A Post-genomic Surprise: The Molecular Reinscription of Race in Science, Law and Medicine," *British Journal of Sociology* 66, no. 1 (2015): 1–27.

"Do Health and Forensic DNA Databases Increase Racial Disparities?" with Peter A. Chow-White, *PLos Medicine* 8, no. 10 (2011): 1–3.

"All That Glitters Isn't Gold" with Osagie Obasogie, *Hastings Center* 41, no. 5 (September-October 2011): 15–18.

"Ancestry Testing and DNA: Uses, Limits—and Caveat Emptor," in S. Krimsky and K. Sloan, eds., *Race and the Genetic Revolution: Science, Myth and Culture*, Columbia U. Press, 2010

"Welcome Freshmen: DNA Swabs, Please," *Chronicle of Higher Education,* May 28, 2010

"Human Genetics and Human Taxonomies: Fluidity, Continuity and Transformations," in *Transforming Racial Images: Analyses of Representations*, Proceedings of the Twelfth Kyoto University International Symposium, Kyoto, Japan, 2009, 81–102

"The Visions and Divisions of American Sociology," with Craig Calhoun and Jonathan Van Antwerpen, in *The ISA Handbook on Diverse Sociological Traditions* (2009)

"Social Issues Lurking in the Over-Representation of Young African American Men in the Expanding DNA Databases," in E. Anderson, ed., *Against the Wall: Poor, Young, Black and Male*, U. of Pennsylvania Press, 2009, pp. 181–197

"The Illusive Gold Standard in Genetic Ancestry Testing," with S Lee, D. Bolnick, P. Ossorio and K. Tallbear, *Science,* July 3, 2009, 38–39

"The Long Path to Higher Education for African Americans," *Thought and Action* 25 (Fall 2009): 99–110

"Race, Genetics, and Disease: Questions of Evidence, Matters of Consequence," with J. H. Fujimura and Ramya Rajagopalan, *Social Studies of Science* 38 (2008): 643–656

"Social and Cultural Implications of Visualizing the Biosciences," in Suzanne Anker and J. D. Talasek, eds., *Visual Culture and Bioscience*, National Academy of Sciences, 2008, 138–139, 167–168

"What Were You Thinking? The Ethical Hazards of Brain Imaging Studies," *Chronicle of Higher Education* 55, no. 7 (October 10, 2008): B4.

"Selective Arrests, an Ever-Expanding DNA Forensic Database, and the Specter of an Early-Twenty-First-Century Equivalent of Phrenology" in Beatriz da Costa and Kavita Philip, eds., *Tactical Biopolitics: Art, Activism, And Technoscience*, MIT Press, 2008 (an earlier version of this appeared by the same title in David Lazer, ed., *DNA and the Criminal Justice System: The Technology of Justice,* 2004, 315–334)

"DNA Dragnets and Race: Larger Social Context, History and Future," in *GeneWatch* 21, no. 3–4 (November-December 2008)

"How to Read a Noose," *Chronicle of Higher Education* 54, no. 11 (November 9, 2007): B24

"Unlocking America: Why and How to Reduce America's Prison Population," with J. Austin et al., The JFA Institute, November 2007

"The Science and Business of Genetic Ancestry Testing," with D. Bolnick et al., *Science* 318 (October 18, 2007): 399–400

"The Medicalization of Race," *The Lancet* 369 (February 24, 2007): 702–704

"The Molecular Reinscription of Race," *Patterns of Prejudice* 40, no. 4/5 (November 2006)

"Explaining Differential Trust of DNA Forensic Technology: Grounded Assessment or Inexplicable Paranoia?" *Journal of Law, Medicine and Ethics* 34, no. 2 (Summer 2006): 293–300

"The Food Issue," with Elizabeth Ransom, *The Nation,* September 11, 2006, 17

"Comparative Perspectives and Competing Explanations: Taking on the Newly Configured Reductionist Challenge to Sociology," *American Sociological Review* 71 (February 2006): 1–15

"Behavioral Genetics and Explanations of the Link between Crime, Violence, and Race," in E. Parens, A. R. Chapman, and N. Press, eds., *Wrestling with Behavioral Genetics: Science, Ethics, and Public Conversation*, Johns Hopkins University Press, 2006

"Engaged Learning Across the Curriculum: The Vertical Integration of Food for Thought," with Alice Waters, *Liberal Education* 92, no. 2 (Spring 2006): 42–47

"Deep Roots and Tangled Branches," *Chronicle of Higher Education* February 3, 2006, B13

"Explaining Increased Racial Conflict in Post-Industrial Societies: The Creation of Systemic 'Competitive' Youth Unemployment," in R. Pinxton and E. Preckler, eds., *Racism in Metropolitan Areas,* Berghahn Books, 2006, 7–22

"Lessons from History: Why Race and Ethnicity Have Played a Major Role in Biomedical Research," *Journal of Law, Medicine and Ethics* (Fall 2006): 487–492

"Race and Reification in Science," *Science,* February 18, 2005, 1050–1051

"Controversies in Biomedical, Behavioral and Forensic Science," with P. Ossorio, *American Psychologist* 60, no. 1 (January 2005): 115–128

"Horizons in Nutritional Science: The Case for Strategic International Alliances to Harness Nutritional Genomics for Public and Personal

Health," with J. Kaput et al., *British Journal of Nutrition* 94 (2005): 623–632.

"The Visions and Divisions of Sociology," with Craig Calhoun, *Chronicle of Higher Education* 51, no. 49: B7

"Feedback Loops in the Politics of Knowledge Production," in Nico Stehr, ed., *The Governance of Knowledge*, 2004, 139–160

"Selective Arrests, An Ever-Expanding DNA Forensic Database, and the Specterof an Early Twenty-First Century Equivalent of Phrenology," in David Lazer, ed., *DNA and the Criminal Justice System: The Technology of Justice,* 2004, 315–334

"The Hidden Eugenic Potential of Germ-Line Interventions," in Audrey R. Chapman and Mark S. Frankel, eds., *Designing our Descendants: The Promises and Perils of Genetic Modifications*, Johns Hopkins University Press, 2003, 156–178

"The International HapMap Project," in Richard A. Gibbs et al., *Nature,* December 18–25, 2003, 789–796

"Buried Alive: The Concept of Race in Science," in Alan H. Goodman, Deborah Heath, and M. Susan Lindee, eds., *Genetic Nature / Culture: Anthropology and Science Beyond the Two-Culture Divide,* University of California Press, 2003, 258–277

"Social Side Effects of the New Human Molecular Genetic Diagnostics," in Michael Yudell and Robert DeSalle, eds., *The Genomic Revolution: Unveiling the Unity of Life*, John Henry Press, 2002

"Sociological Stranger in the Land of Human Genomics," *Contexts* 1, no. 3 (Fall 2002): 69–70

"Medicine, Culture, and Sickle Cell Disease," *Hastings Center Report*, July-August 2002

"Caught Between 'Race' and a Hard Place," *Ethnicities* 2, no. 4 (2002): 547–553

"The Sociology of Science and the Revolution in Molecular Biology," in J. R. Blau, ed., *The Blackwell Companion to Sociology*, Blackwell, 2001

"Race Identity," in N. J. Smelser and Paul B. Baltes (eds.), *International Encyclopedia of the Social & Behavioral Sciences,* Pergamon, 2001: 12703–06

"The Morphing Properties of Whiteness," in B. Rasmussen et al., eds., *The Making and Unmaking of Whiteness*, Duke University Press, 2001

"The Epistemological Challenge of the Early Attack on 'Rate Construction'" *Social Problems* 48, no. 1 (February 2001): 134–137

"Buried Alive: The Concept of Race in Science," *The Chronicle of Higher Education*, September 14, 2001, Section B, 11–12

"A Brief Sociohistorical Odyssey of the American University Through a Lens of Cultural Diversity," in Edgar F. Beckham, ed., *Diversity, De-*

mocracy, and Higher Education: A View From Three Nations, Association of American Colleges and Universities, 2000

"The Social Consequences of Genetic Disclosure," in Ronald Carson and Mark Rothstein, eds., *Culture and Biology*, Johns Hopkins University Press, 1999

"Gefangnis statt Arbeit: Ausgrenzung schwarzer Jugendlicher," in Sabine Lang, Margit Mayer and Christoph Scherrer, eds., *Jobwunder USA: Modell fur Deutschland?* Westfallisches Dampfboot, 1999, 180–191

"An Emerging Reformulation of 'Competence' in an Increasingly Multicultural World," in Bernice A. Pescosolido and Ronald Aminzade, eds., *The Social Worlds of Higher Education*, Pine Forge, 1999, 245–254 (originally published in Rebecca Thompson and Sangeeta Tyagi, eds., *Beyond a Dream Deferred: Multicultural Education and the Politics of Excellence*, University of Minnesota Press, 1993)

"Individual Fairness, Group Preferences, and the California Strategy," in Robert Post and Michael Rogin, eds., *Race and Representation: Affirmative Action*, Zone, 1998 (originally published in *Representations* 55 (Summer 1996): 41–58)

"Persistence and Continuity in Human Genetics and Social Stratification," in Ted Peters, ed., *Genetics: Issues of Social Justice,* Pilgrim Press, 1998, 218–238

"Molecular Halos and Behavioral Glows," in Edward Smith and Walter Sapp, eds*.*, *Plain Talk about the Human Genome Project*, Tuskegee University, 1997, 215–222

"Genetic Information and the Workplace: Legislative Approaches and Policy Challenges," with K. Rothenberg et al., *Science*, March 21, 1997, 1755–1757

"The Quality of the Quantity: Information Technology and the Evaluation of Data," with R. M. Yamashita et al., *Bulletin de Methodologie Sociologique* 54 (March 1997): 123–145

"The Stratification of Cultures as the Barrier to Democratic Pluralism," in Robert Orrill, ed., *Education and Democracy: Re-imagining Liberal Learning in America*, The College Board, 1997, 263–286

"Pattern, Purpose and Race in the Drug War: The Crisis of Credibility in Criminal Justice," in Craig Reinarman and Harry G. Levine, eds., *Crack in America: Demon Drugs and Social Justice*, University of California Press, 1997, 260–287

"What We Can Learn from Other Experiences in Higher Education," in Rachel F. Moran, ed., *Perspectives on Diversity*, Association of American Law Schools, 1997, 33–39

"The Prism of Heritability and the Sociology of Knowledge," in Laura Nader, ed., *Naked Science*: *Anthropological Inquiry into Boundaries, Power, and Knowledge*, Routledge, 1996, 119–130

"The Political Magic of Claims to Neutral Universalisms, Or, 'How to Appear Fair While Converting Substantive Challenges to Political Advocacy,'" in Patricia Meyer Spacks, ed., *Advocacy in the Classroom*, St. Martin's Press, 1996

"It's Just Not Fair," *Ethics and Policy*, Winter 1966, 2–7

"The New Crisis of Legitimacy in Controls, Prisons, and Legal Structures," *The American Sociologist* 26, no. 1 (Spring 1995): 20–27

"Post-Industrialism and Youth Unemployment," in Katherine McFate, Roger Lawson and William Julius Wilson, eds., *Poverty, Inequality and the Future of Social Policy: Western States in the New World Order*, Russell Sage, 1995, 461–486

"The Pluralist Challenge to the Curriculum: A Required Visit to Unexamined Privilege," *Selected Papers from the Texas Seminar on the Core Curriculum*, University of Houston, 1995, 140–145

"The Hidden History of Scientific Racism," *Crossroads* 48 (February 1995): 14–19

"Change and Continuity for Black Students: 1950–1990," afterword to *Head of the Class: An Oral History of African-American Achievement in Higher Education and Beyond*, Twayne Publishers, 1995

"Dépistage génétique et résurgence de l'eugénisme," *Review Quaderni*, Paris, Spring, 1994, 167–182

"Human Genetics, Evolutionary Theory, and Social Stratification," in Albert H. Teich and Mark S. Frankel, eds., *The Genetic Frontier: Ethics, Law and Policy,* American Association for the Advancement of Science Press, 1994

"The 'Violence Initiative' and Scientific Freedom," *The Professional Scholar* 2, no. 3 (April 1993)

"The Diversity of California at Berkeley: An Emerging Reformulation of 'Competence' in an Increasingly Multi-cultural World," in Rebecca Thompson and Sangeeta Tyagi, eds., *Beyond a Dream Deferred: Multicultural Education and the Politics of Excellence*, University of Minnesota Press, 1993

"Genetics, Race and Crime: Recurring Seduction to a False Precision," in Paul Billings, ed., *DNA and Crime: Applications of Molecular Biology in Forensics*, Cold Spring Harbor Laboratory Press, 1992, 129–140

"Understanding Self-Segregation on the Campus," in James I. Brown, ed., *Efficient Reading*, D. C. Heath and Company, 1992 (originally published in *The Chronicle of Higher Education*, September 25, 1991; reprinted segments in Ron Lustig and Jolene Koester, eds., *Intercultural Competence: Interpersonal Communication Between Countries,* HarperCollins, 1992)

"'They're Taking Over' and Other Myths," in *Philosophy and Social Action: Philosophy, Science and Society* 19, no. 1–2 (January 1993):

30–37 (reprinted in Michael Bérubé and Cary Nelson, eds., *Higher Education Under Fire*: *Politics, Economics, and the Crisis of the Humanities,* Routledge, 1995, 276–283; in Kurt Finsterbusch and George McKenna, *Taking Sides: Clashing Views on Controversial Social Issues*, 7th ed., Dushkin, 1992; in *Education: Opposing Viewpoints*, Greenhaven Press, 1992; as "Beyond the Myths," in Patricia Aufderheide, ed., *Beyond PC: Towards a Politics of Understanding*, Graywolf Press, 1992; in *The Writer's Library: Education*, Harper Collins, 1993; originally published in *Mother Jones*, September 1991)

"Assessing the Quality of Life: Genetic Screening, Medical Science and the Backdoor to Medical Eugenics," *Chr. Social Action* 4, no. 1 (1991)

"California as the Future of the Labor Market: Workplace Diversity— Barrier or Opportunity?" with David Nasatir, in M. London et al., eds., *Human Resource Forecasting and Strategy Development*, Quorum Books, 1990, 15–28

"Cross-Cultural Prisms and Trans-Atlantic Mines" (Le Fantome de Frantz Fanon), with David Wellman, *Actes de Récherche en Sciences Sociales* 71 (March 1988)

"Cline's Recombinant DNA Experiment as Political Rashomon," *Politics and the Life Sciences* 6, no. 1 (August 1987): 15–22

"Crime, Youth Unemployment, and the Black Urban Underclass," *Crime and Delinquency* 33, no. 2 (April 1987): 300–315

"Graduate Education at Berkeley," *The American Sociologist* 18, no. 1 (Spring 1987): 83–88

"Purpose and Bias in the Study of Stratified Communities," *Society* 24, no. 2 (January/February 1987)

"Conditions for the Variable Strategies of Cultural Minorities," in *Vers des Societes Pluriculturelles: Etudes Comparatives et Situation en France*, Editions de L'Orstrom, 1987, 516–524

"Priorité de l'emploi et sous-proletariat," *Les Temps Moderne,* December 1986, 214–226

"Social Implications of the 'New' Black Urban Underclass," in Clayborne Carson and Mark McLeod, eds., *Poverty With a Human Face*, Public Media Center, 1985 (reprinted in *The Black Scholar* 19, no. 3 [May/June 1988]: 2–9)

"Political Forces and Biological Science," in *Kagakuasahi, Japanese Journal of Science* 12 (December 1984)

"Alcohol and the Illumination of Social Structure," in Robin Room and Gary Collins, eds., *Alcohol and Disinhibition: Nature and Meaning of the Link*, U.S. Department of Health and Human Services, NIDA Research Monograph 12, 1983, 326–31

"Social Implications of the New Genetics Technology," in *Human Genetic Engineering*, Congressional Record, Sub-Committee on Investigations and Oversight of the Committee on Science and Technology, U.S. House of Representatives, November 1982, 476–500

"Intermediate Steps Between Micro- and Macro- Integration: The Case of Screening for Inherited Disorders," in K. Knorr-Cetina and A. Cicourel, eds., *Advances in Theory and Methodology: Toward an Integration of Micro- and Macrosociologies*, Routledge and Kegan Paul, 1981

"The Ideological Frame of 'Benign Neglect'" in *Journal of Contemporary Studies* IV, no. 1 (Winter 1981): 81–90

"Theories of Race and Social Action," with Herbert Blumer, *Sociological Theories and Race*, UNESCO, 1980

"Moral Philosophy, Or Just a Better Grade?," *American Sociologist* 14, no. 4 (November 1979)

"Field Research and the Protection of Human Subjects," with David Matza and David Wellman, *American Sociologist* 14, no. 3 (August 1979)

"The Structure of Privilege and Its Universe of Discourse," *American Sociologist* 11, no. 2 (May 1976): 73–78

"The Labeling Approach to Deviance," with P. Rains, J. I. Kitsuse, and E. Freidson, in Nicholas Hobbs, ed., *Issues in the Classification of Children*, Vol. 1, Jossey-Bass, 1975, pp. 88–100

"Policy Implications in Social Research," from commentaries in N. J. Demerath, Otto Larsen, and Karl F. Schuessler, *Social Policy and Sociology*, Academic Press, 1975

"Social Desegregation as a Psychological Factor," *Science*, July 6, 1973 (review article of *Black Monday's Children* by G. Powell)

"Conditions for Guilt-Free Massacre," in Nevitt Sanford and Craig Comstock, eds., *Sanctions for Evil*, Jossey-Bass, 1971

"Mental Illness and Criminal Intent," in S. Plog and R. Edgerton, eds., *Changing Perspectives in Mental Illness*, Holt, Rinehart and Winston, 1969

"The Student Role in the Authority System of Higher Education," with Terry F. Lunsford, in *The Encyclopedia of Education*, Vol. 2, Macmillan, 1971, pp. 223–238

"Drugs and Drug Control," in J. Douglas, ed., *Crime in American Society*, Bobbs-Merrill, 1971

"The Third World College and the Colonial analogy," in I. Wallerstein and P. Starr, eds., *The Liberal University Under Attack*, Random House, 1971

"Student Interest, Student Power, and the Swedish Experience," *American Behavioral Scientist* XI, no. 5 (May-June 1968): 21–27 (reprinted in C. Kruybosch and S. Messinger, eds., *The State of the University: Authority and Change*, Sage Publications, 1970)

"Patterns of Deviant Reaction: Some Theoretical Issues," *Social Psychiatry* 3, no. 1 (January 1968): 1–7

"Violence and Desegregation: Combinations of Fear and 'Right,'" in R. Mack, ed., *Our Children's Burden*, Random House, 1968

"The Social Response to Abnormality," *Research Reports in Sociology*, Sociologiska institutionen, Uppsala University, 1963

Major Reports:

Pathways and Barriers to Genetic Testing and Screening: Molecular Genetics Meets the "High-Risk Family," (co-author, Diane Beeson), Final Report to the Director, Office of Energy Research, Office of Health and Environmental Research of the U.S. Department of Energy, October 1997

Desegregation and the Kansas City Missouri School District, Institute for the Study of Social Change, 1994

Making the Future Different: Report of the Task Force on Black Student Eligibility, Office of the President, Kaiser Center, Oakland, California (January, 1990) (one of several co-authors, served as Chair of the Task Force)

The Diversity Project (January 1992) Institute for the Study of Social Change, University of California, Berkeley (one of several co-authors, served as Principal Investigator of the research team and principal author of the report)

Major Recent Book Reviews:

"Review Essay in Symposium on *The Bell Curve,*" *Contemporary Sociology* 24, no. 2 (March 1995): 158–161

Selected Papers Presented at Scientific Meetings:

"Behavioral Genetics, Group Attribution, and Social Stratification," with Aaron Panofsky, *Annual Meetings of the American Association for the Advancement of Science*, February 17, 2002, Boston

"The Political Context of the Attack on Affirmative Action," *93rd Annual Meetings of the American Sociological Association*, San Francisco, August 21–25, 1998

"The Variable Penetration of Genetic Knowledge in High-Risk Populations," *Thirteenth World Congress of Sociology*, meetings of the International Association of Sociology, Bielefeld, Germany, July 20–25, 1994

"The Quality of the Quantity: Information Technology and the Evaluation of Data," with R. Yamashita, H. Besser, T. Piazza, and M. Hout,

Thirteenth World Congress of Sociology, meetings of the International Association of Sociology, Bielefeld, Germany, July 20–25, 1994

Molecular Genetics Meets the High-Risk Family: Close Encounters of Divergent Worlds, *Annual Meetings of the Society for the Study of Social Problems*, Los Angeles, August 4–6, 1994

89th Annual Meetings of the American Sociological Association, Los Angeles, August 4–7, 1994

88th Annual Meetings of the American Sociological Association, Miami, Florida, August, 1993

"Historical Continuities in the Social History of Human Genetic Controversies," *Annual Meetings of the American Association for the Advancement of Science*, Boston, February 15, 1993

"A New and Emerging Conception of Ethnic Diversity," *86th Annual Meetings of the American Sociological Association*, August 23–26, 1991, Cincinnati, Ohio

"The Prism of Heritability and the Sociology of Knowledge," *Annual Meetings of the American Academy for the Advancement of Science*, February 14–19, 1991, Washington, D.C.

"Social Issues in the New Genetics," *Annual Meetings for the Society for the Study of Symbolic Interaction*, August 23–26, 1991, Cincinnati, Ohio

"The Structural Anecdote in Social Analysis," *84th Annual Meetings of the American Sociological Association*, August 9–13, 1989, San Francisco

"Computer Technologies and the Shaping of Social Science Research Methods," with H. Besser, R. Yamashita and D. Wellman, *82d Annual Meetings of the American Sociological Association*, Chicago, August 17–21, 1987

"New Computer Technologies and Research Methods," with H. Besser, Montgomery, Al., July 1987, in *Proceedings of the International Conference on Databases in the Humanities & Social Sciences*

"Computer Technologies and Qualitative Research Methods," with H. Besser and R. Yamashita, *Computers and Qualitative Methods Workshop*, American Sociological Association, Stanford, July 1987

PROFESSIONAL CONSULTATION

Kansas City Legal and Social Options—De-Segregation Plan: Civic Council of Greater Kansas City, Kansas City, Missouri, 1993–94

Workforce Diversity through the Global Scan: American Telephone and Telegraph, Basking Ridge, New Jersey, 1987–90

Community Mobilization for Smoking Cessation: Director of Process Evaluation, Medical Methods Research, Kaiser Foundation Research Institute, Oakland, California 1985–88

Office of Planning and Research: Governor, State of California, 1981

Subdirección General de Planes Provinciales: Departmento de Proyectos y Planificación Rural, Escuela Técnica, Superior de Ingenieros Agrónomos, Madrid, Spain (Research and Consultation on Community Development in Rural Areas of a Developing Nation), 1978–80

Review Panel: National Institute of Mental Health, Center for Metropolitan Studies, Washington, D.C., 1978–80 (member)

Jefferson Associates, Inc., San Francisco: Study of the Impact of the Bay Area Rapid Transit Authority on Institutions and Life Styles in the region, with particular concern for political institutions, 1974–77

Committee on Clinical Evaluation of Narcotic Antagonists: National Academy of Sciences, Washington, D.C., 1973–77 (member)

Review Panel: National Institute on Drug Abuse, Washington, D.C., 1975–77 (member)

National Science Foundation, Washington, D.C.: Review of research grant applications, 1976–78

Russell Sage Foundation, New York: Development of research potential among young social scientists with specialty in problems of inequality between racial and ethnic groups, 1969–71

Pacific State Hospital, Pomona, California: Study of Mental Retardation, 1965

California Rehabilitation Center: Study of social factors in the attempted rehabilitation of narcotic offenders, Norco, California 1963–65

PROFESSIONAL SERVICE

Member, National Advisory Committee, The Decade of Behavior, Washington, D.C., 1998–

Member, Board of Governors, Humanities Research Institute, University of California, 2002–

Member, American Association for the Advancement of Science Committee on Germ-Line Intervention, 1998–2001

Member, National Advisory Council, National Center for Human Genome Research, 1995–

Member, Working Group on Ethical, Legal and Social Issues, National Center for Research on the Human Genome, National Institutes of Health—Department of Energy, 1993–97; Chair, 1996–97

Member, Board of Directors, Association of American Colleges and Universities, Washington, D.C., 1997–

Member, National Panel of the American Commitments Initiative, Association of American Colleges, Washington, D.C., 1993–1996

Member, Committee on Social and Ethical Impact of Advances in Biomedicine, Institute of Medicine, National Academy of Sciences, Washington, D.C., 1991–1994

Member, Special Commission, Meeting the Challenge of Diversity in an Academic Democracy, Association of American Law Schools, Washington, D.C., 1992–1995

Member, Science Advisory Panel, National Institutes of Health, Research on Violence, 1993

Member, Subcommittee on the Protection of Human Subjects, Health and Environmental Research Advisory Committee, Department of Energy, 1994

Executive Office of the Budget, Council of the American Sociological Association, 1991–1993

Council, American Sociological Association, 1988–1991

Corresponding Editor, *Theory and Society*, 1989–1991

Board of Advisory Editors, *Sociological Inquiry*, 1981–1985

Committee on Problems of Drug Dependence, Washington, D.C., 1978–1982

Associate Editor, *Contemporary Sociology*, 1974–1976

Associate Editor, Rose Monograph Series, 1974–1978

Associate Editor, *The American Sociologist*, 1968–1970

PUBLIC SERVICE

Consultant and Advisor, Exploratorium Museum, San Francisco, Interactive Exhibits Programs on Genetics and the Human Genome Project, 1993–1995

Advisory Committee, State of California Master Plan for Post-Secondary Education, 1986–1987

Board of Directors, American College of Traditional Chinese Medicine, San Francisco, 1987–1990

Board of Directors, National Coalition of Universities in the Public Interest, 1985–

Advisory Board, Japanese Pacific Resource Network, 1986–

Board of Directors, Stiles Hall, 1992–1996

Bio-Technology Advisory Council, Joint Committee on Science and Technology, California State Legislature, 1983–1986

Advisory Board, Alcohol Research Group, Berkeley, California, 1986–1996

Board of Directors, Prevention Institute, Marin County, 1988–1991

Advisory Group, Social Science Research Council, Fellowship Program on the Urban Underclass, 1988

South African Career Development and Outreach Program Committee, 1987–1992

Chair, President's Task Force on Black Student Eligibility, University of California, 1986–1990

Principal Investigator, Alameda County Juvenile Delinquency Intervention Project, 1987–1990

National Advisory Board, Center for the Study of Race, Crime, and Social Policy, 1982–1986

Committee on Habitual Behavior and Substance Abuse, National Academy of Sciences, Washington, D.C., 1978–1981

Advisor/Consultant to President's Commission for the Study of Ethical Problems in Medicine, Bio-medical and Behavioral Research, Washington, D.C., 1980

Assembly of Behavioral and Social Sciences, National Research Council, National Academy of Sciences, Washington, D.C., 1973–1978

MAJOR HONORS AND AWARDS

President, American Sociological Association, 2005

Doctor of Science, Awarded by Northwestern University, Evanston, IL, June 2005

Hatfield Scholars Award, 2002

DuBois-Johnson-Frazier Award, American Sociological Association, 2001

Chancellor's Professor, University of California, Berkeley, 1998

Doctor of Letters, awarded by Williams College, Williamstown, Massachusetts, 1991

Ford Foundation, Senior Research Fellow, 1980, Washington D.C.

Research Panel, President's Commission on Mental Health, White House, 1977–1978

Guggenheim Fellow, London School of Economics, London, England 1971–1972

Index

www.ingramcontent.com/pod-product-compliance
Lightning Source LLC
Chambersburg PA
CBHW021822270326
41932CB00007B/300